Adva...
Strengtheni... ...erative
Community

Great job! I love how you weave your long and varied personal experience with cooperatives into your explanation of what cooperatives are and how they have developed. Your recommendations are very thoughtful, reflecting your years of firsthand experience, and make a meaningful contribution to the future of cooperatives. Thank you for taking time to share these insights with the cooperative community and, hopefully, a wider audience.

Charles Gould, former President, International Cooperative Alliance

E.G. has made a major contribution to the history and future impact of cooperative enterprise while at the same time penning an autobiography of a cooperative life well lived. E.G.'s use of real-world stories makes the global impact of cooperatives tangible and personal for multiple audiences, including experienced cooperators.

I hope the 16 recommendations in this narrative will be given serious consideration by cooperative leadership at the global, regional, national and local levels across all sectors. *Strengthening the Cooperative Community* should be required reading for anyone who believes that the future of the globe may be dependent on cooperative thinking and action.

Dr. Martin Lowery, Executive Vice President Emeritus, National Rural Electric Cooperative Association, International Cooperative Alliance board member and Chair, ICA Cooperative Identity Committee.

Nice recap of your cooperative experience, thoughts and research!

Judy Ziewacz, past President and CEO, NCBA CLUSA

With this new "activist" book, E.G. Nadeau has added another treasure-trove of valuable, straightforward advice for cooperatives. E.G.'s own on-the-ground experience highlights a number of the countries where he has worked with cooperatives. This book is a "must-read" for those who want to grow their own cooperative and for those who want to develop more cooperatives.

David J. Thompson, President, Twin Pines Cooperative Foundation

Thank you for this lively, agile, and accessible introduction to the cooperative world, enriched by your experiences gained over many years of practice. In particular, it is interesting to read through the cases of international development cooperation experienced first-hand – how far theory can be from practice and how models need to be translated into concrete contexts to achieve any chance of success. It is a useful reading to approach the cooperative world with realism and without rhetoric.

Gianluca Salvatori, CEO, Euricse

E.G. Nadeau invites us to come along on his career journey studying and working with cooperatives, both in the U.S. and abroad. Reading the book is a surprisingly wide and insightful experience, presented in clear examples, keen observations, and thoughtful lessons.

Michael Sherraden, George Warren Brown Distinguished University Professor; Director, Center for Social Development; Director, Next Age Institute, Washington University in St. Louis

This book is a great resource for those who are just getting started in development or a good refresher for those who have been at it for a number of years. E.G. has done an excellent job of putting together a synopsis of what has worked and not worked during his career in cooperative development.

Todd Thompson, International Development and Cooperative Professional.

Anyone interested in concrete ideas for reducing inequality domestically or internationally should read this book about E.G. Nadeau's 50 years of experience improving economic systems through cooperatives. These ideas can remake capitalism into a fairer system of shared prosperity.

Dave Grace, Managing Partner, Dave Grace and Associates

Thank you for sharing your insights. Overall, I think your book is a good demonstration of the state of affairs back in the 1970s (declining interest in cooperatives; nothing about cooperatives in the curricula) and then the slow resurgence of the subject, thanks not the least to people like you. In this respect, it is very important that this story be told, and lessons be learned, especially in terms of research and education.

Hagen Henrÿ, former ILO COOP Chief and Adjunct Professor of comparative law at the University of Helsinki

You have made an admirable contribution to developing co-operation in the U.S. and around the world, and your reflections are valuable. I particularly liked your take on co-op trade. If the co-operative movement focuses on co-operative to co-operative trade, it can make a genuine contribution.

I also like the idea of co-ops shifting from playing a gap-filler role in a capitalist economy that primarily serves the 1% to instead becoming innovative, proactive leaders in building a more equitable and just world economy.

Tom Webb, President, Global Co-operation, and Adjunct Professor, Sobey School of Business, Saint Mary's University, Canada

Love the content, especially your personal experiences in so many sectors and countries. That gives the book so much credence, and you are such a good writer.

Walden Swanson, Founder and Director Emeritus, CoMetrics

E.G. Nadeau provides readers with a rich memoir of his thinking and experiences in cooperative development in the United States and internationally. Perhaps most useful, he presents a list of recommendations for strengthening and enriching the cooperative community.

Thomas W. Gray, Ph.D., Rural Sociologist/Agricultural Economist, USDA, Rural Development/ Rural Business-Cooperative Service

Your focus on the development challenges to successful co-op development is a valuable contribution. The variety of experiences that you have had during your professional career means that you have much to offer to readers.

Christina Clamp, Professor with the School of Arts and Sciences and Director of Co-operatives and Community Economic Development. Southern New Hampshire University

I enjoy the conversational nature of your writing, unlike academic or industry articles/books that are a challenge to read. You have covered a lot of ground and had many interesting co-op experiences along the way.

Karen Miner, Managing Director, International Centre for Co-operative Management, Sobey School of Business, Saint Mary's University, Canada

I'm impressed with the book and I like your recommendations. This will be a good resource for the staff and members of OCDC, especially lessons learned and strategies that work.

Paul Hazen, Executive Director, U.S. Overseas Cooperative Development Council

I really liked the historical information about the various coop sectors, with multiple examples given from around the world.

Alex Serrano, Senior Vice President for International Programs, NCBA CLUSA

Strengthening
the
Cooperative
Community

Published by E.G. Nadeau, Ph.D.

egnadeau3@gmail.com

thecooperativesociety.org

Madison, Wisconsin

Strengthening the Cooperative Community

E.G. Nadeau, Ph.D.

1. Cooperatives

2. Co-ops

3. Cooperative development

4. History of cooperatives

5. International cooperatives

6. Business model

7. Economic democracy

Other books by E.G. Nadeau:

- *Cooperation Works! How People Are Using Cooperative Action to Rebuild Communities and Revitalize the Economy,* (with David J. Thompson), 1997

- *The Cooperative Solution: How the United States can tame recessions, reduce inequality, and protect the environment,* 2012

- *The Cooperative Society: The Next Stage of Human History* (with Luc Nadeau), first edition, 2016; second edition, 2018

ISBN 978-0-9980662-4-0

Printed in the United States of America

Cover artwork by Luc Nadeau

First printing March 2021

To my grandchildren –
Maia, Alex, Remy, and Hollis

Acknowledgments

I would first like to thank The Cooperative Society Project team for all their help in preparing this book for publication:

Sue Filbin: primary editing, design, and layout

Jill Stevenson: social media and communications

Luc Nadeau: editing, cover artwork, and advice on content and design

Isaac Nadeau: advice on content and design, and coaching

Many people provided valuable help during my co-op career and contributed to the editing of this book. I am grateful to all of them. Key advisers, colleagues, and friends are listed below.

Jim Alrutz, Jim Arts, Liz Bailey, Margaret Bau, Marie-Claude Beaudin, Courtney Berner, Brad Buck; Christina Clamp, Paul Clark, Daniel Côté, Erbin Crowell, Kevin Edberg, Simel Esim, Bill Gessner, Dean Gilge, Charles Gould, Dave Grace, Thomas Gray, Dai Harvey, Paul Hazen, Hagen Henrÿ, Judith Hermanson, Brent Hueth, Andy Lisak, Martin Lowery, Rosemary Mahoney, Zakaria Mamoudou, Leslie Mead, Karen Miner, Mpumelelo Ncwadi, Rod Nilsestuen, Sonja Novkovich, Lynn Pitman, Anne Reynolds, Gianluca Salvatori, Marilyn Scholl, Adam Schwartz, Papa Sene, Alex Serrano, Michael Sherraden, Kate Sumberg, Walden Swanson, David J. Thompson, Todd Thompson, John Torres, Emily Varga, Joyce Wafula, Tom Webb, Gene Wilkening, Ann Woods, Judy Ziewacz.

Table of Contents

Lessons from the History of Cooperatives

Examples of International Cooperative Development

Strengthening the Building Blocks of the Cooperative Community

International Cooperative Growth Opportunities, 2021-2030

Conclusion: Strengthening the International Cooperative Community in the 21st Century

Endnotes

Preface

For the past 50 years, I have had the good fortune of being involved with cooperatives as a researcher, developer, teacher, and writer. This half-century mark is a good time to share some of my experiences and observations related to this democratic business form to which I have devoted my professional life.[1]

The primary purpose of *Strengthening the Cooperative Community* is to provide lessons on the formation and operation of co-ops, co-op support organizations, and co-op-related activities.

The basic approach of the book is to present some personal stories and anecdotes, case studies, and brief essays, and then to draw lessons learned and recommendations on how to strengthen the cooperative movement.

Most of my co-op stories are from the United States and a number of African and Asian countries. That's because most of my career has been spent researching and developing co-ops in these three parts of the world. Many of the examples and lessons drawn from them will be useful in other countries as well.

My hope is that the reader will enjoy the stories and essays, and find the lessons and recommendations useful.

—*E.G. Nadeau, Ph.D.*

Introduction

My first experience with cooperatives

I was fresh out of Harvard in 1970 when I began serving in the Peace Corps in Senegal, a country in West Africa. I lived in Niodior, a fishing village on an island near the mouth of the Saloum River where it flows into the Atlantic Ocean. I dabbled in a variety of community development projects, including latrine and well construction, and the introduction of fertilizers to local crop production. But what interested me the most was trying to figure out a way to help local fishermen market their catches in Dakar, the capital of Senegal, and other cities.

I knew almost nothing about cooperatives at the time, but had a vague notion that they were a means to help groups of people address economic problems. The village fishermen were very good at catching fish, but not so good at selling them.

In pursuit of my interest in learning more about the local fishing system, I tagged along with a group of fishermen on a half-day expedition. We embarked in a large, wooden pirogue (canoe) powered by a Johnson outboard motor. The boat held about eight people and carried a nylon fishing net 100 yards or so in length. After clearing the mouth of the river, my companions scoured the ocean surface looking for ripples that signaled a school of fish below. They then maneuvered the boat to the edge of the turbulent water, turned off the motor, dropped one end of the net over the side of the boat, pulled out their paddles, and quietly, but forcefully, encircled the fish, while playing out the long net. Once the circle was completed, with the boat inside it, they revved up the motor and tore around, scattering the fish into the surrounding net. As they reeled in the net, they plucked hundreds of herring-like fish from it and dropped them into the boat. With just one pass, the boat was full to capacity with fishermen, fish, and me.

On our way back from the fishing grounds, buyers in a large boat took the catch off the fishermen's hands for a nominal price, headed off to the nearest mainland pier, and continued by truck to Dakar or another city to sell the fish to market vendors. The fishermen returned to the village and divvied up their day's earnings in equal shares – one to the owner of the boat, one to the owner of the outboard motor, one to each of the fishermen and, embarrassingly, one to me, who had played the role of deadweight during the trip.

This payment technique was itself a kind of informal cooperation. Why not build on it to develop a cooperative marketing system among the fishermen of the village? They could invest a small part of their earnings in a common fund that would be used to rent trucks and pay drivers to take their fish to urban markets. By skipping the middlemen who currently took their fish and the lion's share of the profits, the fishermen would cooperatively own their own marketing service and share proportionately in the revenue it generated.

So, with the help of a couple of village elders, I convened a large meeting to discuss this idea. My words were greeted politely, but afterward, nothing happened. By the time I left the village at the end of my Peace Corps stint in 1971, nothing continued to happen on the fish marketing co-op front.

In the case of Niodior, there were a number of obstacles between my co-op idea and its realization. I was a young outsider who brashly thought I could convince local leaders to accept a half-baked business idea. My organizing approach was poorly thought out. I might have had a much better chance of receiving a favorable hearing if I had piqued the interest of a small number of key leaders before convening a large meeting. I could have helped to "staff" a steering committee of village leaders as we tried a pilot project, and studied the feasibility, the costs, and the logistics of a fish marketing co-op. The committee then could have brought the results of the research back to the larger group. I did none of these things and, therefore, the project never got beyond the idea stage.

But I was hooked, even if the local fishermen weren't. Although I didn't convince anyone else in the village about the power of co-operatives, I convinced myself. I wanted to learn all I could about co-ops, including how to develop them successfully.

This experience taught me two basic lessons and was the driving force behind my career in cooperatives.

. . . .

Development lessons

I became aware of the huge potential power of cooperatives to solve economic and social problems. Even though my organizing efforts in Niodior were to no avail, I could see how co-ops could increase incomes and social well-being in communities around the world.

I also learned how not to organize a co-op. It's one thing to see an opportunity for cooperative development. It's another thing to turn that opportunity into reality.

In the remainder of this introduction, I provide more information about cooperatives and cooperative development, and describe the organization of the book.

What are cooperatives (often abbreviated as "co-ops")?

A simple definition is that they are businesses that are jointly owned and democratically controlled by the people they serve.

See Appendix A for a more detailed definition of cooperatives and for a presentation of cooperative values and principles. Appendix B provides an annotated list of the different ownership options for cooperatives.

What is cooperative development?

Co-op development refers both to the process of organizing co-ops and to the ongoing activities involved in sustaining them over time. The formation and sustainability of cooperatives are the foundation of a strong, effective, and growing international cooperative community.

In a very real sense, the concept of cooperative development applies to all co-ops, whether they are in the idea stage, in the process of being formed, or in operation. Even co-ops that are decades old can benefit from this development perspective. For example, Daniel Coté has done extensive research on the need for co-ops and credit unions to continually reevaluate how well they are meeting the needs of their members in order to maintain their active commitment and to recruit new members.[2]

Similarly, co-ops exist in different social, economic, and political contexts. An urban neighborhood in a developed country is a very different place from an isolated, rural village in a developing country. These different contexts need to be kept in mind when reviewing cooperative development opportunities. For example, later in the book we shall discuss the role of community solar cooperatives as a means for rural residents who live far away from transmission lines to access electricity.

Why are cooperatives an important business form?

Cooperatives provide a counterpoint to the economic turmoil, wealth and income inequality, and social and environmental degradation caused by for-profit corporations, especially when these corporations are inadequately regulated.

Co-ops play an important role in the world today. There are an estimated three million of them with about 1.2 billion members.[3]

What are the major kinds of cooperatives?

Co-ops are involved in every facet of the world economy, including financial institutions, insurance companies, agriculture, electrical utilities, manufacturing firms, wholesalers, retailers, housing, and service businesses of all kinds. And yet, most people have no idea about the pervasiveness of cooperatives in our lives.

(Please see Appendix B for more information on different kinds of co-ops.)

Further information about cooperatives

If the reader is interested in learning more about the array of co-ops and their role in the larger economy and society, I've listed several online resources in this endnote.[4]

Organization of the book

The remainder of *Strengthening the Cooperative Community* is divided into four sections: an historical review of major co-op sectors; brief case studies of recent international co-op development successes and failures; analyses and recommendations related to the building blocks of co-op development; and recommendations for realizing future cooperative development opportunities.

Lessons from the History of Cooperatives

My Peace Corps experience was a case study of what not to do in forming a co-op. Where better to look for how to do it right than from historical examples? History provides a rich trove of information on co-op successes and failures.

It is almost a truism to write that learning from the history of co-ops is an excellent way to increase the likelihood of forming and sustaining successful cooperatives in the future. Unfortunately, during the course of my career, I have found far too many instances in which co-op development initiatives have ignored the lessons from past successes and failures, and have suffered the consequences.

One chronic example of this is the pattern of designing short-term projects (1-5 years) and providing short-term funding for long-term cooperative development initiatives. This is a recipe for failure that continues to be repeated by co-op development organizations and their public and private funders, despite all of the historical examples warning about the problems of this approach.

Precursors of formal co-ops

Joseph P. Knapp, a well-regarded co-op historian, cites the Pilgrims in Plymouth, Massachusetts, as the first cooperative community in the New World. (Not unexpectedly, this example focuses on European settlers, and doesn't mention the cooperative activities of the migrants from Asia who arrived in the Americas about 15,000 years earlier.) Around 1600, this religious community organized a cooperative approach to agriculture. Community members farmed on large tracts of land, performing many activities collectively – land clearing, fencing, planting, etc. – but maintained separate control over family parcels for care of crops and animals.[5]

My own ancestor, Joseph Osanni Nadeau, arrived in Canada in 1661, and took up farming the next year on Ile d'Orleans, not far from the city of Québec.[6] The island was divided up into about 300 linear parcels that reached from the St. Lawrence River to the central part of the island. The location of the farming settlement on an island was in large part for defensive purposes, to protect the residents from attack by Native Americans. Similar to the Pilgrims, there were probably also a wide range of informal cooperative activities among these settlers in addition to shared protection.

I would characterize cases like these as precursors of formal co-ops, because they were not contractually based organizations with specific sets of rules and principles – especially related to democratic control and the priority goal of service to members.

The emergence of formal cooperatives

Formal co-ops began to emerge about 400 years ago in Europe.

Mutual insurance (a type of cooperatively organized insurance) came first, beginning around 1700, followed more than a century later by consumer goods co-ops, financial co-ops (including credit unions), and agricultural co-ops. The broader co-op movement didn't take off until early in the 20th century when these sectors expanded rapidly. New sectors, especially rural electric, telephone, and water utility co-ops in the United States, emerged in the 1930s and '40s; worker-owned co-ops, especially in the Basque region of Spain and in the Emilia Romagna region of Italy, developed after the Second World War; and social co-ops became a significant force in Italy, and to a lesser extent elsewhere in Europe, beginning in the 1980s. *(See Appendix B for basic information about these co-op sectors.)*

This section of the book looks at historical examples of the rise and spread of different cooperative sectors and activities, and lessons derived from varying paths of development.

The cases focus on seven co-op sectors: mutual insurance, consumer goods, finance, agriculture, rural electrification, worker-ownership, and social services.[7] The historical reviews are presented in chronological order, based on when the earliest co-ops in each category emerged. Following the sectoral examples, there is a chapter on the history of cooperative development, and a chapter comparing the different strategies used in co-op development.

Chapter 1

Fighting Fires in Philly

Benjamin Franklin, mutual insurance organizer

Franklin is known for many things: as a prominent Philadelphia printer, a scientist (remember the famous experiment in which he flew a kite with a key attached in a thunderstorm to test his theory about electricity?), and a signer of both the U.S. Declaration of Independence and the Constitution.[8]

But Franklin is less well-known as a co-founder of the Philadelphia Contributionship for the Insurance of Houses from Loss by Fire. Formed in 1752. It is considered to be the oldest mutual insurance company – and the first formal co-op – in, what was to become, the United States. The company is still in existence today.[9]

Following is an excerpt from Franklin's autobiography, referring to a paper he wrote on reducing the incidence of fires in Philadelphia:

> *This was much spoken of as a useful piece and gave rise to a project which soon followed it, of forming a company for the*

more ready extinguishing of fires and mutual assistance in removing and securing of goods when in danger … The utility of this institution soon appeared, and many more desiring to be admitted than we thought convenient for one company, they were advised to form another, which was accordingly done; and this went on, one new company being formed after another … I question whether there is a city anywhere in the world that is better provided with the means of putting a stop to beginning conflagrations. [10]

Urban-based mutuals

Mutual insurance is cited as the oldest kind of formally organized cooperative business. [11] It developed during the early years of the Industrial Revolution both in Europe and in North America. Beginning in the late 1600s and the 1700s, pooling risks against the ever-present danger of fires in rapidly expanding cities, mostly built of wood, made a great deal of sense. Neighborhood fire brigades and these early mutuals represented collective strategies for both reducing fire risk and damage, and rebuilding after fires occurred.

In the United States, mutual Insurance companies developed from the bottom up. The first insurance law in the country was enacted in New York in 1849, well after many mutual insurance companies were already in operation. [12]

Westward Ho

There was a lag between the formation of urban mutuals and their rural counterparts in the United States. The first rural companies were organized by farmers in New England beginning in the 1820s. As settlers moved west, they formed additional companies. By 1860, there were an estimated 100 mutuals located from Maine to Missouri. [13] The National Association of Mutual Insurance

Companies was formed in 1895. By 1920, the number of companies had increased to about 2,000. The growth in mutual fire insurance companies was accompanied by consolidation, expansion, and diversification. The total number of policyholders grew exponentially.[14]

Characteristics of mutuals

The extension of mutual protection to health, life, and, beginning in the 20th century, automobiles and other vehicles, was a logical expansion of coverage for these companies. All of these types of insurance removed some of the uncertainty from everyday life for individuals, families, and businesses.

Although mutual insurance companies are often defined as cooperatives, it is important to note several characteristics of these companies that are different from other cooperatives.

"Membership" in a mutual insurance company is defined differently. Instead of buying a share of voting stock or paying a membership fee, one becomes a member-owner of a mutual insurance company by becoming a policyholder. Major decision-making is based on the principle of "one policy, one vote."

Another characteristic of mutuals that is different from most other co-ops is "proxy voting" in which policyholders can choose to have the board of directors cast votes on their behalf. In practice, this usually means that the directors of mutuals have a lot more decision-making power than those of most other cooperatives.

Thus, many mutual insurance policyholders are not aware of the fact that they own and, at least in theory, democratically control their insurance companies.

Mutual insurance today

A recent survey indicated that there are approximately 1,500 mutual insurance companies in the United States with combined memberships of about 233 million individuals, families, and businesses. [15]

On a global scale, there are more than 5,000 mutual insurance companies with more than 900 million memberships.[16] Mutual insurance companies have by far the largest number of memberships of all the co-op sectors and do about one-fourth of all the insurance business in the world.

. . . .

Development lessons

Protection of one's home, business, and neighborhood from fire (as well as safeguarding health, life, property, and vehicles) are powerful motivators for cooperation.

Mutual insurance is an example of a kind of co-op that originally grew from the bottom up and from experiences shared from one community to the next.

Despite their humble beginnings, some of the largest co-ops in the world are mutuals. They now have more members/policyholders and a more highly integrated international network than any other type of cooperative.

Chapter 2

Willy Street and Other Grocery Cooperatives

The Rochdale Society of Equitable Pioneers is considered by most in the co-op community as the first successful consumer goods co-op. It was founded by a group of weavers in Manchester, England, in 1844. Their cooperative store stocked small quantities of food and other household items.[17]

There was a scattering of other consumer goods cooperatives in England that formed during the early and mid-1800s. Many failed, in part, because of their lack of clear guiding principles. Rochdale not only survived, but became a model for other co-ops. In fact, there is a direct line of descent from this single co-op to the entire consumer co-op movement in the United Kingdom today. Democratic ownership and member returns based on the value of purchases from the co-op were two of the key principles that Rochdale introduced.

Willy Street Grocery Co-op

My membership number at Willy Street Grocery Co-op is 168. This small number means that I joined the co-op back in 1974 during its first couple of months of operation. Since then, about 100,000 individuals and families have become members.

The co-op (named after Williamson Street on the near east side of Madison, WI, which in turn is named after Hugh Williamson, one of the signers of the U.S. Constitution), has grown from a small store, with a limited number of grocery items, to three supermarkets in the Madison area, specializing in organic and other healthy foods and products. Throughout this growth, the co-op has retained its commitment to its members and to the community.[18]

National Co+op Grocers

Willy Street is part of a unique group within the U.S. cooperative community. The 1960s and early 1970s were characterized by unrest among young people in the United States and in other countries, about the war in Vietnam, race relations, poverty, and other issues. One of the major themes of the day was: "Question Authority." A wave of hundreds of natural foods co-ops was formed across the U.S. as part of this movement. Two common themes among them were providing healthy, often locally grown, food and commitment to community.

During the past five decades, these co-ops have undergone a lot of changes. Some have gone out of business. The ones that survived have matured tremendously as businesses while retaining their focus on healthy food and healthy communities. For the most part, they have experienced major expansions, and, in many cases, established additional stores.

Willy Street, along with about 150 other retail food co-ops, is a member-owner of National Co+op Grocers. "NCG helps unify natural food co-ops in order to optimize operational and marketing resources, strengthen purchasing power, and ultimately offer more value to natural food co-op owners and shoppers everywhere." NCG's retail food co-op members "operate over 200 stores in 38 states with combined annual sales over $2.1 billion and over 1.3 million consumer-owners."[19]

These and other U.S. food co-ops provide an excellent example of a relatively small group of businesses having a significant impact on an entire sector of the economy. The University of Wisconsin Center for Cooperatives concluded in a report from 2009:

> The leadership role of these co-ops in the food industry
> is especially apparent in the way that they and a relatively
> small number of organic farmers and food companies
> have dramatically increased the availability of organic
> foods in the marketplace during the past 40 years.[20]

Migros and The Co-op dominate retail food sales in Switzerland

Willy Street and the other co-op owners of National Co+op Grocers represent a decentralized model of consumer goods co-ops. Migros and The Co-op are examples of centralized cooperatives with many local branches. Together these two supermarket co-ops dominate the Swiss retail food market.[21] (This is somewhat surprising given that Switzerland is considered by many to be the bastion of international capitalism.)

Grocery co-ops today

The number of grocery co-ops in the United States is relatively small – estimated at a little over 300 with a total membership of about 2 million, including both NCG and non-NCG co-ops.[22]

Internationally, these numbers are dramatically higher, with about 80,000 co-ops and 100 million members.[23]

. . . .

Development lessons

Once a set of broadly agreed-upon principles were established – especially democratic control and patronage-based refunds – consumer goods co-ops took off.

There are multiple models for successful consumer goods co-ops, including local freestanding co-ops and groups of affiliated co-ops as well as large, centralized examples.

Food co-ops in the U.S. have had a big impact on their economic sector without having a large share of the market in that sector.

Chapter 3

Not Having to be Rich to Save and Borrow

Origins of financial cooperatives

The first financial cooperatives were separately developed in the mid-1800s by two Germans – Friedrich Wilhelm Raiffeisen and Franz Hermann Schulze-Delitzsch. Both of these men were motivated by the lack of access of most individuals and small businesses to affordable credit and places to safeguard their savings.[24]

From Germany, a variety of financial co-op models spread elsewhere in Europe and then to Canada and the United States. As with the grocery co-ops discussed in the previous chapter, financial co-ops evolved in two different directions – large centralized organizations and smaller, mostly locally based entities. For example, Crédit Agricole, headquartered in France, is the largest financial co-op (and the largest co-op) in the world.[25] On the other hand, there are thousands of credit unions in the United States and Canada, mostly serving individual communities and affiliated groups of members.[26]

Following is a brief case study of the development of credit unions in the United States.

Edward Filene and Roy Bergengren, credit union champions in the United States

In the early 20th century, U.S. banks did not show much interest in the savings and borrowing needs of middle- and low-income Americans. Credit unions played the lead role in filling this gap.

As with mutual insurance, financial cooperatives were first developed in Europe. In the case of credit unions, the model was imported to Canada and then to the United States. French Canadian residents started the first U.S. credit union in Manchester, New Hampshire, in 1909.

At about the same time, the banking commissioner of Massachusetts carried out "an investigation into the operations of professional moneylenders who are victimizing factory workers in Boston." This investigation led to the passage of a credit union law in Massachusetts in 1909, the first such law in the country.[27]

Edward Filene, who is best known for the Boston department store chain that bore his family's name, was also a philanthropist who focused his attention on the wellbeing of the employees of his own company and working people in general. Filene was a strong supporter of the 1909 Massachusetts law and, more importantly, in 1921 donated a million dollars for the start-up of the Credit Union National Extension Bureau, a private, non-profit entity, whose mission was to lead a national movement for the formation of credit unions.[28]

Filene hired the attorney Roy Bergengren to manage the Bureau. These two men launched a highly successful strategy for credit union development. As Bergengren told the story:

> *We agreed on the first day that the Bureau had four objectives. ... Our first objective was to make it possible, by adequate legislation, to organize credit unions anywhere in the United States. ... [The] second objective involved the organization of individual credit unions until the plan had been popularized and methods of credit union mass production had evolved. The third objective looked forward to permanent, self-sustaining state leagues of credit unions which would, in each state, take over the local direction of credit union development. Finally, it was our purpose, from the beginning to organize the Credit Union National Association as a national union of credit unions ... and turn over to the Association when organized, the permanent direction of the cooperative credit movement in United States. ...*[29]

And, that's exactly what happened during the next two decades. The number of credit unions in the United States increased from 190 in 1921 to 1,300 in 1930 to 9,200 in 1940. During that same time period, memberships increased from 72,000 to 2.7 million. Thirty-three state credit union leagues formed the Credit Union National Association in 1934.[30]

The number of credit unions in the United States peaked at about 24,000 in 1969 with a total membership of 22 million. Since then, there has been a great deal of consolidation among credit unions, with the total number of memberships continuing to grow.

Current status

According to the U.S. National Credit Union Administration, at the end of 2019 there were 5,236 federally insured credit unions in the United States with a total membership of a little more than 120 million.[31]

The latest data on credit unions around the world indicate that there were 85,400 at the end of 2018, with about 275 million memberships.[32]

An international review of co-ops published in 2014 estimated that the combined number of credit unions and other cooperative financial institutions totaled about 210,000, with a combined membership of a little more than 700 million.[33] These numbers indicate that financial cooperatives are the second largest co-op sector after insurance mutuals.

. . . .

Development lessons

The U.S. credit union movement grew dramatically beginning in the early 1920s, with significant growth in membership continuing a century later. The success of these co-ops is primarily due to a number of factors:

- Meeting the need for savings and borrowing by middle- and low-income members

- Private philanthropy (especially the financial support of Edward Filene)

- The passage of state credit union laws

- The establishment of state-level "leagues"

- The formation and ongoing support of the Credit Union National Association

Both the decentralized model of credit unions in the U.S. and other parts of the world, and more centralized financial cooperative models in Europe and other countries, have proven to be successful.

Chapter 4

Trust-busting Farmers

Agricultural cooperatives provide a means for farmers to purchase inputs, receive services, and sell farm products through organizations they own and democratically control. Farmer co-ops emerged in the second half of the 19th century in Europe and North America. In the past 70 years, they have also become an important means for improving agriculture and farmers' incomes in developing countries, for example in India and Brazil.[34]

A strong impetus for the development of these co-ops was countering the control of agricultural markets by large corporations. Farmers often paid exorbitant prices for inputs (seeds, fertilizers, farm implements, and other necessities of farming) and transportation; borrowed money at high interest rates; and lacked bargaining power in the sale of farm products such as grains and livestock.

Farmer woes in the post-Civil War United States

As I wrote in *The Cooperative Solution*, published in 2012:

> In the late 1800s and early 1900s, farmers and ranchers accounted for about 40% of the American workforce. They were dependent on a range of other businesses to supply them with agricultural inputs and to transport and purchase their crops and livestock. These agriculture-related businesses had an unfair advantage over dispersed, small farmers in negotiating prices for these various services.[35]

Historian Joseph Knapp elaborated on this theme:

> [The farmer] blamed much of his plight on an unfair system of "interchange," whereby he was forced to pay

excessive toll in marketing his products, and excessive prices for his purchased supplies; and he was vehement in his resentment of all "monopolists" and "middlemen." As the farmer saw his condition, he was 'fleeced both coming and going.' Unable individually to protect himself against exploitation from industry which was rapidly becoming organized in corporations and combinations, the farmer turned for relief to economic cooperation as a counter method of organization....[36]

Sunkist

For example, after the transcontinental railroad system was completed in 1869, California citrus growers struggled for more than three decades to gain control of the shipment of their fruit to eastern markets. These growers had to figure out a way to counter the power of middlemen and to organize growers.

The solution was through the formation of the California Fruit Growers Exchange, which developed a strong marketing strategy in 1903.[37] This cooperative, now known as Sunkist, "is the oldest continually operating citrus cooperative in America and the largest marketing cooperative in the world's fruit and vegetable industry."[38]

Establishing fairness

For decades, farmers struggled to form business organizations to level the playing field. By the 1920s, they had formed successful cooperatives in many states to provide these services for themselves or to negotiate with farm-related businesses for fairer prices and other concessions.[39]

About a third of all farm supplies and agricultural products in the U.S. are purchased and marketed through cooperatives.[40] Even in areas where cooperatives account for a relatively small percentage of agricultural business activity, their presence in the marketplace makes a difference because competitors know that if they charge too much for farm inputs or don't pay enough to purchase farm products, there are co-ops that can step in and outcompete them. [41] [42]

The post-Civil War focus of most efforts at agricultural cooperation was in the north and the west among small- and medium-size white farmers. For almost 50 years, most agricultural organizing efforts were failures. Farmers were not able to develop effective strategies to counter the economic power of the companies that controlled agricultural markets.[43]

I wrote in *The Cooperation Solution*:

> In the development of U.S. agricultural cooperatives, it is important to note that their eventual success resulted both from broad-based action by farmers across the country and from federal legislation. In the late 19th and early 20th centuries, there were many agricultural cooperative failures. This difficult start-up period was due to a variety of factors, including the economic strength of the supply, transport, and marketing businesses the farm organizations were up against as well as ineffective business models and under-financing of many of these early co-ops.[44]

> The 1920s began with a severe post-World War I agricultural depression. Farm organizations, especially the American Farm Bureau Federation, the National Farmers Union, and the National Grange, were able to make their voices heard in Washington, D.C., on both sides of the political aisle because of their strong base of support within the agricultural community and because of the severity of the agricultural depression.

> In 1921, representatives of these farm organizations met in Washington to identify legislation that could address farm credit, transportation, legal, and other issues related to co-ops. Following this meeting, agricultural leaders ...

assembled a number of Republican and Democratic senators from the farm states and got them to pledge themselves to support legislation necessary for the welfare of agriculture. This was the genesis of the "Farm Bloc" which was to exert great political power during the next few years.[45]

Five federal laws were passed between 1914 and 1929 that helped set the stage for a dramatic increase in the number and strength of farm co-ops during the next two decades:

- The Smith-Lever Act of 1914, which formalized the U.S. Department of Agriculture's extension system, including training and development assistance for farmer co-ops[46]

- The Federal Farm Loan Act of 1916, which provided badly needed credit to farmers and farm co-ops (and was the precursor to today's farm credit cooperatives)[47]

- The Capper-Volstead Act of 1922, which permitted agricultural co-ops to coordinate the marketing of products without running afoul of anti-trust laws

- The Cooperative Marketing Act of 1926, which broadened the ability of agricultural co-ops to share information and marketing activities

- The Agricultural Marketing Act of 1929, which established the Federal Farm Board and provided various means to strengthen and stabilize the prices of agricultural products[48]

The primary reason to list these federal programs here is to underscore the combined role that farm organizations, working at the national level, and the federal government played in launching a strong agricultural cooperative movement in the United States that continues to this day. [49]

Current status

In 2016, the U.S. Department of Agriculture estimated that there were about 1950 agricultural cooperatives in the United States with approximately 2 million members.[50]

A recent estimate for the number of agricultural co-ops on a world scale is about 1.2 million with a combined membership of 122 million.[51]

. . . .

Development lessons

Developing an effective strategy for taking on the concentrated economic power of supply, marketing, and transportation businesses was a long and difficult battle, hindered by poorly organized co-ops and the strength of the opposition.

Anti-trust legislation and the establishment of cooperative development assistance programs at the federal level played a key role in the eventual success of these co-ops.

Chapter 5

Filling the Rural Energy Vacuum in the United States

Both rural electric cooperatives and credit unions were launched and had major periods of expansion in the United States during the first half of the 20th century. A similarity in the development of the two co-op sectors is that for-profit banks showed little interest in addressing the financial needs of middle- and low-income borrowers, and for-profit electric power utilities showed little interest in serving rural communities.

However, there was a major difference in the development strategies of these two consumer co-op sectors.

Credit unions grew rapidly after 1921 due to a combination of private philanthropy (notably by Edward Filene), a well-orchestrated national organizing campaign, and strong grassroots involvement.

Rural electrics, on the other hand, had a more complicated start-up that involved decades of farm organizations lobbying for federal action, which resulted in the passage of the Rural Electrification Act (REA) in 1936.[52] As with credit unions, the subsequent rapid growth of electric co-ops was due to grassroots support, which, among other activities, included door-to-door canvassing by volunteers to get the number of customers required to make local electrification feasible.

A key difference between the two cooperative sectors was that credit unions were inexpensive to start up. Rural electrics were far more capital- and labor-intensive because of the need to develop or access sources of electric power and transmit electricity over large, sparsely populated areas.

REA addressed the problem of capitalization by providing long-term, affordable loans to organizations that undertook rural electrification projects. The initial bias of Morris Cooke, the first REA administrator, was to have established power utilities take the lead in rural electrification. But, despite Cooke's efforts, the private utilities shunned the program. In fact, they initiated a boycott of REA in late 1935.[53]

Despite this opposition, in the first five years of the program, from 1936 through 1940, there were over 1,300 borrowers of REA funds, 90% of which were cooperatives.[54] These initial utilities funded by REA were serving almost 1 million customers by the end of 1940.

In effect, private power utilities decided that it would not be profitable for them to serve rural America and ceded most of the field to rural electric cooperatives.

Current status

In 2020, electric cooperatives in the United States provide energy services to 42 million people in 47 states.[55]

Internationally, there are electric cooperatives in dozens of countries. However, there is not a clear estimate of the total number of people and organizations who receive electricity through them.

. . . .

Development lessons

Rural electric co-ops were successful in the United States for four main reasons:

- High demand for electricity by farmers and other rural residents

- Lobbying the federal government by farm and other rural organizations

- The establishment of the Rural Electrification Administration, a federal program, that provided financial assistance to rural energy projects

- A lack of interest by established, urban-oriented private utilities

Chapter 6

Employees Running Their Own Businesses

Union Cab

In the late 1970s, there was a strike at one of Madison's taxi companies. Rather than settling the dispute, the owner sold his cabs to another company, leaving his employees high and dry. In response, some of the former employees developed a business plan for a new cab company which they would own as a worker co-op. The big sticking point was sourcing start-up capital for this new venture.

Fortuitously, the city had just formed and provided financing for the Madison Development Corporation (MDC), an entity established to assist a variety of economic projects with potential benefit to the community. I was one of the initial board members of MDC. We jumped at the chance to support this start-up by providing a subordinated loan that enabled the fledgling company to secure a much larger conventional loan from a local bank.

More than 40 years later, Union Cab is still thriving in Madison as the city's largest taxi company. A recent report indicates that the co-op has about 250 members and more than 80 cabs, almost all of which are hybrid electric Priuses.[56]

Mondragon

Mondragon is the most famous employee-owned cooperative federation in the world. In the 1950s, José María Arizmendiarrieta, a young Catholic priest who taught at the technical high school near the city of Mondragon in the Basque region of Spain, was the primary strategist for, and organizer of, a manufacturing business owned by its employees. Over the years, a network of additional businesses and related organizations was added to this worker co-op federation. According to Mondragon's 2018 annual report, more than 80,000 employees, almost 75% of whom were member-owners,[57] worked for the affiliated 260 individual businesses in the co-op network.[58]

In the 1950s, Mondragon and the rest of the Basque region was in the midst of an economic depression brought about by the Spanish Civil War and the continued animosity of the Franco regime. What the co-op federation effectively did was to create an array of inter-related co-op businesses and service organizations that stimulated the local economy, launched successful affiliated businesses, and provided support services to local residents.

For example, if a group wanted to form a new worker co-op, they developed a business plan with the technical support of Mondragon's business consultants. If the plan appeared feasible, it could receive financing from the co-op network's credit union. Then, the network would continue to provide technical assistance to the new worker co-op to increase the likelihood that it would be successful. Not only that, the co-op network has a technical school that provides well-trained employees for its co-op member companies. If there are layoffs in one of the businesses, the network reassigns the unemployed workers to other businesses or to further training, followed by re-employment in a network business.[59] This integrated support system has been somewhat weakened since Spain joined the European Union, largely because of limitations imposed by the European Bank.[60]

Current status

Worker co-ops represent a very small portion of the U.S. economy. Community-wealth.org estimated that there were 394 worker co-ops in the United States in 2017 with about 6,700 employees.[61]

In contrast, a UN-sponsored study, published in 2014, concluded that there were about 85,000 worker co-ops around the world with well over 1 million employee-owners.[62] Most of these co-ops are concentrated in European Union countries and South America.[63] Compared to other types of co-ops, these are still relatively small numbers.

. . . .

Development lessons

Worker co-ops can save jobs in local communities by keeping businesses in operation that would otherwise close down or relocate.

Mondragon is a model, not only for organizing a federated group of worker co-ops, but also for providing an array of coordinated services to new and established worker co-ops.

Isolated, small workers co-ops like Union Cab can also succeed in the marketplace as long as they have good business plans and adequate financing.

Chapter 7

Organizations That Meet Human Needs

"Social enterprises are organizations that address a basic unmet need or solve a social or environmental problem through a market-driven approach."[64] They can be organized as for-profits, nonprofits, or cooperatives. This type of organization has become far more numerous in the past three decades. This chapter focuses on social enterprises that are organized as cooperatives.

Italian social cooperatives

The earliest social co-ops in Italy were formed in the late 1970s. In 1991, the Italian government established an official status for these cooperatives, divided into two main categories: "Co-ops that carry out activities in the area of health, social or educational services; and co-ops that act as agencies for integrating disadvantaged people in the labor market."[65]

The Italian law also stipulates membership rules regarding these co-ops. Some have workers as members, others have a mix of workers, consumers and/or trainees, and some have a membership category for investors. By 2017, there were about 16,000 cooperatives registered under the 1991 law.[66] In many communities, these co-ops have become an important part of the service network. For example, a recent study indicated that the city of Bologna contracts for about 85% of its social services through these co-ops, including childcare, eldercare, and a wide range of other services.[67]

Social enterprises in other countries

Since the official recognition of the Italian social cooperatives, many other European Union members – including Belgium, France, Ireland, Poland, Slovakia, and Spain – have established statutes for social enterprises. There are approximately 430,000 social enterprises in the E.U., many of which are organized as co-ops.[68] There are also well-established, social enterprise movements in Japan and Canada.[69] These social enterprises, including social co-ops, have greatly expanded a business model that puts social, community, and environmental services above profits.

Social co-ops in the US

Although there are many social enterprises in the United States, few are organized as social co-ops. The most prominent examples are housing cooperatives for the elderly – usually organized as consumer co-ops, and worker cooperatives that specialize in home-care services.

Growing pains

Despite the rapid growth of social enterprises in the past three decades, they are still at an early stage in the development of a consistent business model. Three of the most important steps in furthering this model will be to: have an agreed-upon definition of what is, and what is not, a social enterprise; establish clear, consistent legislation for social enterprises, including social co-ops, in both developing and developed countries; and create transparent means to measure and report on their performance in achieving social, community, and environmental objectives.

Current status

As mentioned above, there are a relatively small number of social co-ops in the United States, but the possibilities for future growth are excellent.

The European Union has invested far more resources than the United States in analyzing and promoting social enterprises. According to a report published by the European Commission in January 2020, "There are 2.8 million social economy enterprises and organisations, ranging from SMEs (small- to mid-size enterprises) to large EU groups. Together, these enterprises employ 13.6 million citizens and account for 8% of the Union's GDP." Although the report identifies different kinds of social enterprises, it does not provide a definitive number for social co-ops.[70]

According to the United Nations Secretary General Report on Cooperatives in Social Development (2017), the social economy contributes about 7% to the world's gross domestic product (GDP) and to global employment.[71] Again, however, the report does not provide a clear breakout of the number of social co-ops.

. . . .

Development lessons

The passage of a social co-op law in Italy was a critical factor in creating a rapid and consistent dissemination of this approach to social services.

Social co-ops and other social enterprises are filling a need that is not being met by government or traditional service businesses. As a result, the number of these co-ops in Italy and other countries appears to be growing exponentially.

Italian social co-ops include a variety of models of "multi-stakeholder" cooperatives that are owned by workers, consumers, and investors. These models provide valuable information for other co-op sectors in which multi-stakeholder options may be used.

Chapter 8

A Historical Look at How Cooperatives are Formed

The seven previous chapters reviewed the historical origins and current status of a number of major cooperative sectors. As we saw, co-ops have had a long and diverse history, beginning with mutual insurance companies that formed in the late 1600s and 1700s, and continuing with a wide array of other sectors, including relative newcomers such as worker co-ops and social co-ops.

This chapter describes the evolution of development assistance across cooperative sectors. That is, it focuses on the support system for co-ops and co-op formation, rather than the sector-by-sector growth of co-ops.

Co-op organizing efforts prior to 1895

Prior to the inauguration of the International Cooperative Alliance (ICA) in 1895, most attempts to form new co-ops occurred within co-op sectors, within individual countries, and/or originated from a variety of uncoordinated, sometimes poorly thought-out, business strategies. Such independent, co-op-organizing efforts still occur, but most co-op initiatives involve some level of coordination with, or at least knowledge of, the broader co-op movement.

Some of the early co-op development attempts in Europe and the United States ended in failure – for example, hundreds of poorly conceived and operated agricultural co-ops during the latter half of the 19th century.[72] But others were very successful, and set the stage for thousands of co-ops that are thriving today. Insurance mutuals, financial co-ops, and some consumer goods co-ops come readily to mind as examples of such long-term, successful development efforts.

Cooperative development in the 20th century

The establishment of the International Cooperative Alliance in 1895 marked a key turning point in the growth and integration of the cooperative community. As never before, cooperative leaders saw themselves as part of one large movement that represented a range of economic and social sectors. However, the establishment of this single, worldwide apex organization did not translate immediately into more systematic approaches to cross-sectoral cooperative development.

In the United States, the formation of the Cooperative Extension Service by the U.S. Department of Agriculture in 1914 had a big impact on the establishment of cooperatives, especially agricultural supply and marketing co-ops. The active organizing role of co-op extension agents, jointly employed by the U.S. Department of Agriculture and Land Grant Colleges[73] such as the University of Wisconsin-Madison, continued into the 1960s. This type of assistance decreased after that, to a significant degree because large agricultural co-ops no longer needed it. Other co-op sectors such as mutual insurance, credit unions, and rural electrics had matured and formed their own apex and support organizations. This left a vacuum in which those interested in forming new co-ops – in specialty farm products, healthcare, housing, grocery stores, taxi companies, childcare, and many other areas – had limited sources of assistance to turn to for help.

In Europe, the pattern of sector-specific, and country-specific, cooperative development continued to be the norm for most of the 20th century. It is important to note that Europe faced far more conflict during the century than did the United States, especially the two world wars and the divisive effects of the Cold War. The European Union was not formed until 1993.[74] Co-op Europe, a regional entity of the International Cooperative Alliance, was not established until 2005.[75]

In Japan, the consumer co-op movement began in the late 1800s, influenced by the early British co-ops. However, the Japanese Consumers Cooperative Union did not see rapid growth until the 1970s, well after the Second World War.[76] The Japan Workers' Cooperative Union was founded in 1979, consolidating efforts to form worker co-ops in the face of extremely high unemployment in the country.[77]

With a few exceptions, cooperatives grew relatively slowly in other parts of the world until after World War II. In addition to the establishment of Co-op Europe in 2005, the Asia-Pacific region of the International Cooperative Alliance was formally established in 1960,[78] the Africa region in 1968,[79] and the Americas region in 1990.[80]

The growth of cooperative development organizations in the United States

As mentioned above, the U.S. Department of Agriculture began to provide domestic cooperative development assistance through its Cooperative Extension Service in 1914. Within the cooperative community itself, however, the first comprehensive, cooperative development assistance was targeted to other countries rather than to communities in the U.S. The National Cooperative Business Association, the apex organization of U.S. cooperatives, began providing such assistance in India in 1953.[81]

The first domestically oriented cooperative development organization (CDO), the Federation of Southern Cooperatives, wasn't formed until 1967 as part of the War on Poverty. The Federation is headquartered in Epes, Alabama, and serves nine Southern states. Its mission is to "collectively support and advocate for Black farmers and rural communities across the South through economic development, training, policy advocacy, and organizing."[82]

The second domestically oriented CDO was formed in Wisconsin in 1985. Because I was closely involved with this organization for almost 30 years, and because it set the stage for a national network of CDOs, I provide a brief case study of its formation and operation below.

Setting the stage for the formation of Cooperative Development Services

In the 1970s and early 1980s, the Wisconsin Federation of Cooperatives (WFC) provided organizing assistance to a variety of new co-ops, including Group Health Cooperative of South Central Wisconsin (now a nationally recognized health maintenance organization) and the Western Wisconsin Communications Cooperative (the first rural cable TV cooperative in the United States and a pioneer in distance learning). This co-op merged with Tri-County Telephone Co-op in 2006 to become Tri-County Communications Cooperative.[83]

However, these co-op development activities were an awkward fit for this dues-based, cooperative trade association. It was hard to justify using members' dues to assist start-up co-op projects that were not in a position to support the Federation. On the other hand, the need for co-op development assistance was clearly present. A Cooperative Development Summit was convened in 1982 by the Federation, at which the idea for separate, self-supporting cooperative-development organizations (CDOs) gained traction. Creating such an entity in Wisconsin would relieve the Federation of the cost and responsibility for providing cooperative-development assistance but, at the same time, co-op assistance needs would be met.

In January 1985, I was hired by Rod Nilsestuen,[84] the Executive Director of the Wisconsin Federation of Cooperatives (WFC), to be the organizer of the Wisconsin Cooperative Development Council. Six months later we incorporated this new organization. By the end of the year, the Council had raised enough public and private seed funding to begin operation.

I served as the director for seven years until the Council merged with North Country Cooperative Development Services and was re-named Cooperative Development Services, Inc., (CDS) with an expanded mission to serve Minnesota and Iowa (and other states as opportunities arose) as well as Wisconsin. I worked at CDS as an employee and consultant until 2013.

Start-up and growth

To keep things simple, I will refer to the Council/Cooperative Development Services as CDS. The first issue to address is: How did CDS get from the idea stage to a functioning organization?

The biggest factor in this transition was the sponsorship of CDS by the Wisconsin Federation of Cooperatives, especially the ability to benefit from Nilsestuen's leadership within the cooperative community – both at the state and national levels – and his good relationship with both Republican and Democratic government officials.

A cooperative development organization such as CDS is unlikely to make big money on fee-for-service contracts with well-heeled clients. Most of the new cooperatives that the organization helps to develop (or discourages from forming because they are unlikely to succeed as profitable businesses) are generally not in a position to pay for business planning, market studies, and other development services.

Established co-ops that seek out assistance from CDS are often looking for help because of financial difficulties and, thus, are also unlikely to be able to pay much for troubleshooting assistance. Large co-ops, for example, in agriculture, energy, and credit unions, are unlikely to make use of the services of an organization such as CDS because they have their own sources of technical assistance within their sectors.

The upshot of all of this is that for CDS to go into business, it needed to have significant financial support from public and/or private sources. We developed a two-pronged strategy in 1985 and early 1986 to capitalize the organization: paving the way for an appropriation from the State of Wisconsin, and organizing a fund-raising campaign among major regional and national cooperative organizations.

To set the stage for these two campaigns, in the summer of 1985 we incorporated the organization as a cooperative containing a charitable fund (which was eligible for tax-deductible contributions)[85] with a board of directors representing a cross-section of state and national co-op-related organizations.

We were lucky that the governor of Wisconsin called a special legislative session on economic development in the fall of 1985. With the lobbying leadership of WFC, we were able to have CDS included among a dozen or so economic-development initiatives considered at that session. The legislature voted overwhelmingly to provide $180,000 to CDS on the condition that we were able to raise an equal or greater amount of funds from non-governmental sources.

This victory set the stage for the second prong of our funding strategy. We were then able to approach large organizations within the cooperative community with requests for funding that would double the impact of their donations. In large part because of Nilsestuen's leadership, we raised well over $180,000 from large, co-op-related donors.[86] Most of the donations were spread over a three-year period to make it easier on the funders.

CDS benefited from the fact that it was intended to fill a gap in co-op development assistance that had been left by the gradual withdrawal of extension services from this activity. It also took a burden off the shoulders of WFC.

. . . .

Development lessons

This is not a startup strategy that every cooperative development organization can use. However, there are elements of it that can be adapted by many of them:

- Seeking organizational, financial, and lobbying support from established cooperative organizations

- Structuring themselves to be able to access tax-deductible donations and grants

- Basing their development strategy on a combination of public and private financial support, and fee-for-service payments from clients

The startup strategy worked. We began hiring professional staff and providing development services in early 1986. Between 1986 and 2020, CDS has carried out hundreds of projects, and continues to do so.

At the outset, we weren't sure what types of co-op projects we would be assisting. We knew that there was a lot of interest in start-up co-ops, but we didn't know which ones we would be working with. In fact, our clients were and are very diverse – including daycare centers, farmer groups, worker co-ops, credit unions, forestry initiatives, and many other entities.

We ended up providing most of our development assistance to food-related projects, in particular specialty agricultural co-ops and natural foods co-ops. And, surprisingly to us, we ended up staffing and co-staffing two multi-state initiatives – one called the Midwest Organic Alliance and the other The Food Alliance. The former project coordinated farmers, processors, and grocery stores to certify and promote organic food products. The latter was also oriented toward healthy-foods certification and marketing with an emphasis on the reduced use of agricultural chemicals.

Our work with natural foods co-ops began in our first year of operation because of the leadership of Walden Swanson and Kate Sumberg, two of our lead co-op developers. This work accelerated in 1992 when we merged with North Country Cooperative Development Services. As a result of the merger, Bill Gessner, another prominent foods co-op developer, became a consultant to CDS. His contacts with a range of food co-op consultants led to the formation of a subgroup within CDS that specialized in food co-op consulting. This subgroup became the preeminent co-op consulting group in natural foods in the United States.

By mutual agreement, the natural foods consulting group split off from CDS in 2008 and created a separate service cooperative that is now called Columinate. The consulting co-op continues to thrive. As its website states:

> With over 40 consultants, Columinate is a national consulting cooperative serving mission-driven organizations, including food co-ops, electric co-ops, healthcare organizations, credit unions, schools, and nonprofits.[87]

··

Development lesson
Sometimes, the best way to increase the impact of CDOs on expanding and improving the quality of co-op business services is to re-organize, in this case creating a second co-op service organization.

Cooperative development organizations successfully lobby for federal funding

As mentioned earlier in this chapter, cooperative development organizations (CDOs) generally need to be subsidized by public and/or private grants in order to be effective. After all, they are not looking for wealthy clients, but rather those who need financial assistance or low-cost technical assistance in order to launch, expand, or improve the performance of their co-ops.

Successful fundraising has been, and continues to be, a necessary, ongoing activity to supplement the organization's fee-for-service income.

In the late 1980s, there were only a handful of CDOs in the country, all in search of more stable sources of funding. Working with the National Cooperative Business Association and the Cooperative Development Foundation, this group of CDOs and other cooperative organizations devised a strategy to secure ongoing financial support from the U.S. Department of Agriculture. The group formed a national task force, led by Nilsestuen, to lobby Congress for a minor change in language in an already existing provision of the Farm Bill. The proposed modification provided a category of funding for rural cooperative development. The lobbying effort was successful, and in 1990 the Rural Cooperative Development Grant Program was established.

As the USDA website states:

> The Rural Cooperative Development Grant Program
> improves the economic condition of rural areas by

helping individuals and businesses start, expand or improve rural cooperatives and other mutually-owned businesses through Cooperative Development Centers. Grants are awarded through a national competition.[88]

This program has provided a few million dollars annually (the exact amount has varied from year to year) for which rural CDOs could apply for funding. Grants have generally been in the $150,000 to $300,000 range. Although by no means a guaranteed source of funds, the availability of these grants has provided some degree of stability for CDOs across the country. In essence, the existence of this program helped to transform a few scattered experiments in rural cooperative development into a national movement during the 1990s.

The formation of CooperationWorks!

The informal group of CDOs that began meeting in the late 1980s continued to meet and grow in number during the next two decades. In 1999, nine CDOs formed a nonprofit network with the name CooperationWorks![89] There are now about 35 such organizations serving all 50 states. This is quite a change from when there were only two CDOs in the entire country in 1985.

To quote from the CooperationWorks! website:

> [We are] a national network made up of organizational and individual members working in cooperative development. Our members provide everything from board trainings to business planning for new and growing co-ops.[90]

Concluding comments on the growth of cooperatives

The cooperative community has come a long way since the formation of a few fire insurance mutuals in the late 1600s and 1700s. This chapter has provided an historical perspective on how this growth has evolved over the past 300-plus years. Cooperative development organizations were given special attention in the chapter as a relatively new approach to expanding and sustaining co-ops around the world.

Chapter 9

Lessons from the Historical Review of Cooperatives

This section of the book has provided historical examples of the origins and growth of different cooperative sectors and of the evolution of the co-op development process itself.

This chapter identifies both some common themes and some different patterns of growth and failure across these examples. How do co-ops get started and proliferate? What lessons can we learn about how to develop and maintain successful co-ops in the future – and how to reduce co-op failures?

Reasons for success

The development of successful cooperatives has a number of common themes:

- Adequate demand for a set of goods or services – often a demand that was ignored or downplayed by for-profit businesses

- A clear set of principles – especially democratic control by members and allocation of surplusses to members based on patronage of the co-op rather than shares of ownership

- Champions who fervently believe in the potential of a co-op idea and effectively acted on their beliefs

- The feasibility of the co-op as a business – that is, in the realistic potential of it to provide a set of goods or services at a profit

- Adequate capitalization – sources of equity and debt capital to launch and maintain the co-op until it can turn a profit

- Competent managers and directors who both understand how to run a business and are committed to the co-op principles

- Members who are committed to buying from, selling to, and/ or working within the cooperative, not merely for their own short-term benefits, but for the long-term good of the co-op

Different paths to successful development

These themes can be seen as a common foundation for most successful cooperatives. However, there are significant variations, in particular, as they relate to co-op development in different sectors. Some co-ops started up and grew rapidly at a national or international level because of strong, widespread demand for previously unmet needs.

Other co-ops faced greater impediments to formation and growth such as high capitalization costs or a market dominated by large competitors. They needed government regulatory or financial support to gain traction.

There are co-op sectors that serve relatively small numbers of members but have had a disproportionately large impact on the economic sectors in which they operate.

Mutual insurance companies and credit unions are two classic examples of cooperatives that thrived based on visionary leadership, strong demand by consumers, low capitalization costs, supportive legislation, and a model for development that was easily transferable from one community to another.

In the United States, agricultural and rural electric cooperatives were formed based on a different development model. They resulted from partnerships between advocacy organizations, consumers or producers, and the federal government, which provided legislative and financial support. In the case of farm co-ops, both antitrust protection and access to affordable capital were prerequisites to long-term success. In the case of rural electric cooperatives, the Rural Electrification Act was critical to providing affordable financing for a capital-intensive industry.

The "new wave" food co-op movement that began in the late 1960s in the United States provides an unusual example of a grassroots development approach that has had very little government support. At the same time, however, these co-ops and their members played a strong leadership role in the passage of the Organic Food Production Act of 1990. This act created certification standards for organic foods that affected the entire food industry.[91]

Worker co-ops are an example of a kind of cooperative that has often developed with little or no governmental assistance. In fact, the premier federation of worker co-ops in the world – Mondragon in the Basque country of Spain – emerged and thrived beginning in the 1950s, in part as a reaction to the Franco regime. Thus far, worker co-ops have had virtually no federal support and only a minor presence in the United States.

Also in the United States, social co-ops have generally operated with little governmental support. In contrast to the U.S., Italy has a national law legitimating a role for social cooperatives. Many local units of government contract with these cooperatives for services.[92]

. . . .

Development lessons

Historically, cooperatives have been established in a variety of ways, including freestanding initiatives by small groups, mutual support and learning by example, coordinated development within cooperative sectors, government assistance, and technical and financial support from cooperative development organizations.

At the same time, cooperatives share many similar attributes, as listed near the beginning of the chapter.

The primary lesson from this comparison of approaches to cooperative development across sectors is that there is no single pattern that characterizes their successful development.

As Chapter 34 elaborates, both domestic and international cooperative-development organizations appear to be an increasingly promising means for growing and strengthening the cooperative community in the 21st century.

Examples of International Cooperative Development

After receiving my Ph.D. in sociology at the end of 1977, my career was focused primarily on cooperative development in the United States for almost the next quarter-century. However, my interest in co-ops began in Africa, and I had always hoped to get back into cooperative development and research on that continent.

In 2000, I was invited by Jim Alrutz, Africa Director for the National Cooperative Business Association's CLUSA program,[93] to do a consultation in Zambia and make some recommendations about the agricultural co-ops being formed there by CLUSA. This was 27 years after my dissertation research on farmer co-ops in the same country. The assignment in Zambia was one of about 25 international co-op research and development projects that I carried out over the past 20 years.

This section contains 18 stories, all but one of which are about my cooperative adventures in Eastern Europe, Africa, Asia, and the Caribbean, and some of the major lessons I learned from them. The stories are mostly in chronological order, beginning with a project in Poland in 1991. I deviate from a strictly chronological approach because I worked in some countries – including Ghana, Kenya, Sri Lanka, and South Africa – several times, and wanted to group projects that were interlinked.

The one project recounted in this section that I didn't visit is a long-term cooperative initiative in Indonesia and East Timor. I included it because of the unique, successful development model it represents.

Chapter 10

Cooperative Evaluation Project in Poland – 1991

With the break-up of the Soviet Union in the late 1980s and early 1990s, former Soviet Bloc countries were exploring what to do with the economic disarray they faced domestically and their changing roles in the international arena.

One of these countries was Poland. The U.S. Agency for International Development (USAID) provided funding in 1991 to Volunteers for Overseas Cooperative Assistance (VOCA)[94] and other organizations to help the fledgling Polish government review its economic options.

I was hired as a volunteer to spend a month in the Radomsko area of central Poland to visit agricultural, worker, consumer, and multi-stakeholder cooperatives, and prepare a report on how these co-ops might fit into post-Soviet Poland. Altogether, I visited about 25 co-ops. My conclusion was that some of them – in particular, some worker, consumer, and multi-stakeholder co-ops in the retail goods sector, and some agricultural supply and marketing co-ops – had very good potential to adapt to the new economy. I recommended that others, such as some agricultural equipment and services co-ops, should probably be closed down.

I remember attending a conference at the end of my stay, in which a law professor from the United States essentially wrote off all the co-ops in the country, and proposed a new co-op law, modeled after co-op laws in the United States. I thought how tremendously narrow-minded and shortsighted his perspective was. But, this kind of biased and half-baked analysis won the day, because, like many new regimes, the Polish government was very willing to throw the baby out with the bathwater, even if it meant significantly slowing down the economic rebirth of the country. Thus, my careful case-study research and conclusions were for naught. The co-ops I thought worth saving were thrown out with the bathwater.

....

Development lessons
Beware of experts who blindly apply development prescriptions that are out of context.

Beware of political leaders who are more interested in change for change's sake than in careful, strategically-based development.

Chapter 11

Developing an Agricultural Marketing Strategy in Zambia – 2000

My three-week assignment in Zambia was to provide advice on two agricultural co-op projects – one in central Zambia near the capital, Lusaka, and the other near Chipata in Eastern Province. Both of these projects worked with small farmers, organizing them into primary and secondary co-ops. Primary co-ops were usually at the village level, and secondary co-ops at the multi-village level.

CLUSA wanted to organize a third-level co-op in the Chipata area that was intended to help the farmers' groups become more effective at marketing their groundnuts and other cash crops. This third-tier entity was referred to as a producer-owned trading company (POTC). It was my job to make suggestions on how this new organization should be structured.

There were several problems in attempting to organize a trading company in the Chipata area. These included the lack of a strong commitment to the primary and secondary co-ops by local farmers; difficulty in attracting a talented manager to Chipata; and inadequate capital by the POTC to purchase products from the farmers and market them effectively.

In addition, several private trading companies were buying products directly from farmers,[95] thus undercutting the role of the primary and secondary co-ops in generating higher revenue for farmers and operating revenue for the co-ops.

I was to learn over the years that this problem of "side selling" is a common one for farmers and co-ops in many developing countries. Private buyers often paid less than the co-ops, but they tended to pay in cash or barter at the time of purchase. They also had a pattern of buying when farmers were most economically vulnerable, that is when their reserves of food and money were low – around the beginning of the planting season. Another tactic was to loan money or sell inputs, often at exorbitant rates, if the farmers promised to sell their products to them during the harvest season.

CLUSA staff worked with the POTC board of directors to help counter these problems, but the deck was stacked against them. Despite the difficulties with the trading company, it is important to note that this project and the one in the Lusaka area did make an important difference for local farmers by helping them to get involved in cash crops and thereby improve their incomes.

To conclude this chapter, not much changed in agricultural practices by small farmers between my 1973 research in Zambia and my 2000 visit. The vast majority of Zambians were still farming at a subsistence or a "subsistence-plus" level. Many of the farmer groups I saw in 2000 were facing similar problems to the poorly functioning agricultural co-op I studied in 1973: insufficient resources, and difficulties in effectively using the power of cooperatives to purchase inputs and sell agricultural products.

One thing that was just beginning to change in 2000, with the help of CLUSA, was the adoption of "conservation farming." This is a set of agricultural practices designed to maximize production on both small and large farms by preparing the soil and applying mulch and fertilizer near the end of the dry season, and by planting properly spaced seeds in time to catch the first rains of the rainy season. These practices often result in doubling production compared to traditional farming methods.[96]

. . . .

Development lessons

In order to be successful, third-level co-ops require primary and secondary co-ops that are well-managed and have loyal members who buy from, and sell to, their co-ops.

Private traders used a variety of tactics to outcompete the POTC at buying cash crops from farmers. One way to increase the effectiveness of third-level co-ops is for the co-op development organization to provide long-term technical and financial support. See Chapter 27 for CLUSA's approach to doing this in Indonesia and East Timor.

Chapter 12

An Effort to Rebuild Ghana's Cooperative Movement – 2002-2004

Ghana had a detailed cooperative law and a thriving, albeit British-dominated, cooperative movement during its colonial incarnation as the Gold Coast. The core of that co-op movement was cocoa marketing – still Ghana's largest export.

Kwame Nkrumah, the first president of Ghana, was an important leader in the African liberation movement of the 1950s and '60s. Like many of his peers, one of his primary goals was to consolidate and retain power in his own country. Unfortunately, much of the cooperative infrastructure was a casualty of domestic political infighting in the early years after independence. In particular, Nkrumah consolidated government control over cocoa marketing and displaced the cocoa cooperatives, the backbone of the country's co-ops.[97]

Thus, the context for my consulting work in Ghana was the legacy of a broken co-op movement. Part of this legacy was that there continued to be a national council of co-ops with a largely geriatric group of board members who presided over a movement that was a shell of its former self. There were a couple of sectors – especially credit unions and alcohol production co-ops – that were active and thriving. For the most part, however, including in agriculture, there was little co-op activity.

An exception to the lack of successful cooperatives in agriculture was Kuapa Kokoo, a large co-op that specializes in certified fair trade cocoa. It was formed in 1993 and claims about 100,000 members.[98] It is also a part owner of Divine Chocolate, that markets chocolate bars in Europe and North America.[99]

My first assignment in Ghana in 2002, coordinated by Papa Sene, the regional coordinator for CLUSA in West Africa, was to conduct a training program for about 100 government-employed, co-op extension staff from around the country. I got the impression that the trainees were not well-versed in the co-op development opportunities in their areas of the country, and had limited support in their work from the Department of Cooperatives. This impression was supported when I was on a consulting assignment in the field a couple of years later. A government-employed co-op resource person had no interest in assisting me to identify agricultural co-ops in his service area unless I paid him – under the table – for doing so. Fortunately, I found a committed, honest extension agent to work with.

A second activity was to advise the council staff and board on a strategy for revitalizing co-ops in the country. A major part of that strategy was to seek out funding from USAID, the World Bank, and other donors to carry out one or more agricultural co-op development projects. These efforts proved fruitless, despite the excellent potential for producer co-ops in Ghana.

A third activity in which Papa Sene and I collaborated was to work with Ghanaian co-op members on developing a revised co-op law for the country. I will discuss this legal reform project in Chapter 32. But to give a brief preview, the process of developing a new draft co-op law went very well, but lobbying the Ghanaian government to adopt it did not. Ghana continues to rely on a paternalistic, colonially drafted co-op law, the most recent version of which dates back to 1965.[100]

· ·

Development lessons

It's very difficult to resurrect a co-op movement from the top down. Without a strong base of support, co-op leaders are negotiating with government agencies and potential donors from a position of weakness.

In some cases, government-employed co-op development agents can lose sight of their missions, and, without being held accountable, are not a force for positive co-op change.

The lack of support for cooperatives by Ghanaian political leaders was illustrated by the fact that they showed no interest in reforming the paternalistic co-op law of the country.

Chapter 13

Evaluation of an Agricultural Co-op Project in Mozambique – 2004

In 1975, after a protracted 10-year war of liberation, Mozambique gained independence from Portugal, which, as a colonial ruler, had been far more interested in extracting agricultural and other wealth than in educating Mozambicans and assisting in economic development. From 1977 to 1992, this fledgling country also had to deal with a quasi-civil war which in many ways was part of a proxy war between white-ruled Rhodesia and apartheid South Africa on one side, and the newly minted self-ruled countries in southern Africa on the other. The civil war took a huge social and economic toll on Mozambique.

CLUSA's co-op development assistance in Northern Mozambique began in 1995, when the country was just beginning to emerge from civil war. The focus of its work was to develop agricultural cooperatives in order to get the country on the road to food self-sufficiency.

My job was to do an evaluation of the project to see how well CLUSA was carrying out this mission in 2004, and whether or not it made sense to provide the project with another round of USAID funding. My overall assessment was a positive one. Something like 25,000 farmers were involved in the network of pre-cooperatives that CLUSA had helped to launch – pre-co-ops, because Mozambique did not have a workable co-op law. As is often the case with agricultural organizations in developing countries, the farmers proved much more adept at growing crops and raising livestock than they were at marketing them. But things were improving.

CLUSA was attempting to establish a third-tier entity in Mozambique to help address this marketing problem. As in Zambia, they called the third-level organization a producer-owned trading company. In Mozambique, the trading company was legally structured as a limited liability company primarily owned by GAPI (a government-owned financial company) and OXFAM (an international nonprofit organization). The POTC in Mozambique faced many of the same problems as its counterpart in Zambia, especially side selling to private buyers and weak management.

After conducting some field research, which showed that several crops were going to fall short of their targeted production levels, I met with the manager of the trading company who provided me with a marketing plan for the year. This plan showed that the crops that were underperforming were still listed as major export items for the year by the trading company. It turned out that the marketing plan had not been updated from the beginning of the year, and therefore did not reflect the current reality regarding the level of performance of different crops. Thus, it was useless as a market-planning tool.

Other nonprofits undercutting CLUSA's agricultural development efforts

An ironic problem that I encountered while doing my research was that some international nonprofits were undercutting the development work of other nonprofits. For example, CARE, a nonprofit that was formed with the assistance of the cooperative movement in the United States shortly after World War II, was still in a "feed the people" mode of operation rather than a "help the people feed themselves" mode. The result of these conflicting approaches to assistance was the creation of a mentality among some Mozambican farmers that they should continue to rely on handouts rather than using outside assistance to develop their own agricultural production.

One consequence of this dependency pattern was that some farmers treated CLUSA's agricultural loans as gifts. This "handout" mentality resulted in a low loan repayment rate. Thus, the donor nonprofits created a culture of dependency that was difficult for the development-oriented nonprofits to overcome. What's worse was that some non-profits were still fostering this mentality at the same time that the CLUSA project was in the process of building self-sufficiency.

Another big problem was the difficulty of organizing co-ops in a young country that did not have a good cooperative law. The project could still organize "cooperative-like organizations," but it couldn't register them with the government as co-ops. So, CLUSA had to wage a lobbying effort with the Mozambican government at the same time that it was playing an agricultural cooperative development role.

. . . .

Development lessons

CLUSA showed that it was possible to do large-scale organizing of farming cooperatives in a country that had just been ravaged by civil war.

Nonprofit organizations can sometimes be an impediment to cooperative development by creating a handout-based mentality among farmers and undercutting economic development. The CLUSA project was able to thrive despite this problem.

Mozambique's lack of a good cooperative law made it more difficult to organize clear, rules-based co-ops. Again, CLUSA was able to develop co-ops in this environment and even contribute to the improvement of the cooperative law of the country.

Chapter 14

Historical Review of a Health Initiative in Burkina Faso – 2006

In the early 1990s, CLUSA carried out a health project that was intended to establish village-level health committees and secondary clusters of these committees organized around government health clinics to provide coordination and communication across villages. The project was funded for only three years, and then was supposed to be turned over to the Burkina Health Ministry to continue as part of its outreach program.

CLUSA's Africa staff in Washington, D.C., were very interested in seeing how this program was faring 10+ years after they had handed the ball off to the Burkina Health Ministry. I was hired to review the current situation by overseeing a survey of about 60 regional health centers, and conducting face-to-face interviews in 16 of them. Papa Sene, the West Africa regional director for CLUSA, worked with me on carrying out the research and writing up the report.

The results of that research can be summarized quickly. Virtually nothing remained at the primary village level from the project CLUSA left behind in 1994. However, many of the secondary health committees continued to function effectively, especially in the oversight of their clinic-level pharmacies.

The main reason for the demise of the primary health committees was that the Health Ministry effectively dismantled the program in 1995. CLUSA had trained seven employees of the Ministry as community facilitators to work with village groups in developing, implementing, and revising health plans. Within a year after CLUSA's departure, all seven facilitators had been reassigned to other jobs. In all the villages we visited, only two had active primary health committees. Interestingly, neither of these committees were part of the original program from the early 1990s.

After CLUSA's departure and the reassignment of the community health facilitators, the standard procedure was for Health Ministry staff to hold a meeting once a year in each village and essentially tell the residents what their local health priorities would be in the coming year, rather than asking them for input on local health concerns. In fact, there was a standardized "village health plan" that was signed off on by the leadership in each village. This was basically a rubberstamp process rather than genuine input.

For example, in Burkina Faso, malaria is a big problem in some villages and not a problem at all in others, depending on the local habitat for mosquitoes, especially the amount of standing water. But in the "rubberstamp" approach to measuring village health, all the villages had malaria listed as a priority problem. Thus, for example, villages that were located far away from health clinics would not have the opportunity to list access to a clinic as a major issue.

At the secondary level, where the clinics were located, the situation was better. The multi-village health committees played an important role in overseeing the operation of the community pharmacies.

UNICEF had provided a basic stock of medicines and other health-related items to these pharmacies in the early '90s. The program was designed to be self-sustaining. That is, the pharmacies charged a small amount for drugs and other items purchased from them. These funds were reinvested in more health-related products. This cycle was intended to be continued on an ongoing basis. Amazingly, 14 of the 16 community pharmacies were still in operation when we visited them in 2006. What appeared to make the pharmacy program successful was that the multi-village health committees took their oversight role seriously, and stayed committed to the self-financing of the pharmacies. I should also add that the staff of the local health clinics also benefited from the continued operation of these pharmacies because their patients had ready access to prescriptions and other health purchases. (It's also worth noting that the temptation to "raid" the tills of these pharmacies was minimized because of health committee oversight.)

. . . .

Development lessons

Three years is a very short time period in which to organize a large-scale, community health program that is intended to be long-term and self-sufficient. A strong case can be made for not only having longer development periods for projects like this, for example five years or more, but also for continued monitoring and incentives after the main development and implementation part of the project has been completed.

Burkina Faso's Health Ministry does not appear to have had a commitment to continue the program after CLUSA left. In fact, the reverse may be true. Village health committees may have been seen as an added burden and, perhaps, a complicating factor in determining local health priorities. This could explain the Ministry's effective termination of the village-level program within a year after CLUSA's departure. If there had been some type of ongoing incentive to reward regional clinics for supporting village committees, the outcome might have been very different.

The continued operation of most of the community pharmacies that we visited more than 10 years after the completion of the CLUSA program constitutes a huge success. It appears to reflect the value of a self-financing model with community oversight.

Although the village health committee model did not work out well in Burkina Faso, primarily because of the short duration of the CLUSA project and the lack of commitment from the Ministry of Health, the basic strategy of primary village health committees linked to secondary committees appears to be a good way to get villagers involved in their own health planning and care. As we shall see in Chapter 16, CLUSA's community-based healthcare project in Kenya, that lasted over a decade in the early 2000s, exemplifies a successful long-term project.

Chapter 15

An Evaluation of Mutual Health Insurance in West Africa – 2007-2008

This project was categorically different from any of the other international consultancies that I participated in during the past 20 years. Some of the key differences:

- It was a comparative analysis of community health insurance programs across three neighboring countries – Mali, Burkina Faso, and Benin.

- The primary research methodology was to conduct site visits and interviews in 30 different communities – 10 in each country.

- The goals of the project were to evaluate community health mutual insurance programs, to learn from their successes and failures, and to develop new approaches to community health-care based on research results.

The project was also the most intense and exhausting research project I participated in as an international consultant. My colleagues and I drove over 6,000 miles, often on potholed, gravel roads during a six-week time period as we traveled from interview site to site.

What we discovered in this odyssey was mostly disappointing. In general, these "community health mutuals" were not community-based, did not provide health services to very many people, and were not "mutually" or democratically run.

As the *Guide to Cooperative Approaches to Community Health*, prepared by the CLUSA team after the field research, concluded:

- Minimal community participation took place during the initial design and establishment of the mutuals. Indeed, in all but three of the communities visited, the goal of forming a mutual came from outside the community, and in almost all cases, recommendations in the outsiders' feasibility studies were adopted without changes.

- None of the communities carried out research prior to establishing the mutual to determine the health needs and priorities deemed most important by community residents nor whether a mutual would meet those needs.

- Few mutuals had undertaken long-term strategic and financial planning.

- A majority of the mutuals provided insurance services to less than 5% of their communities.

- In more than half of the mutuals, 50% or more of beneficiaries were not current in their payments.

- In 25 of the 30 mutuals, the role of paid staff was filled by often temporary and less-trained volunteers.[101]

. . . .

Development lessons

There was a fundamental flaw in the design of most of these health mutuals. Simply put, they were financially unsustainable, because local residents were unable or unwilling to pay the monthly dues required for services. Fairly basic community surveys and business plans would have concluded that most of these mutuals would be infeasible, and that the organizers should not have proceeded with their development.

So, why didn't these upfront feasibility analyses take place? Starkly put, it was not in the interests of the mutual organizers to conduct them. Their primary goal was to establish an agreed-upon number of community health mutuals, come hell or high water. Proceeding on the basis of careful feasibility analyses would have interfered with this goal because fewer mutuals would have been established.

This same type of disconnect between organizer goals and sustainability also affected the low level of community involvement in most of these mutuals. Grassroots organizing takes time and effort, and also requires a level of responsiveness by the organizers to community residents. This type of time-consuming, careful community involvement was not in the interest of the organizers, and, thus, did not occur in most instances.

A more fundamental issue here is the questionable vetting and monitoring process of project developers by funders. For example, USAID put a lot of money into a U.S.-based, for-profit corporation, for the development of community health mutuals in Africa.[102]

During the course of my international development work, I occasionally encountered approaches to development, including "cooperative" development, that were ill-conceived and not in the best interests of the recipients of the assistance. Most of the mutuals in this study fall into this category.

Despite the problems mentioned above, CLUSA was able to produce a guide to the formation of cooperatively-oriented community health organizations that showed how to avoid many of the shortcomings identified in the study.

Chapter 16

Chronicling a Community Health Model in Kenya – 2009-2011

I had the opportunity to evaluate a successful, community-based healthcare program in Kenya during several trips there between 2009 and 2011. This was a refreshing change-of-pace after research on the two mostly unsuccessful healthcare initiatives reviewed above, one in Burkina Faso in which the Ministry of Health effectively terminated a promising village-level model started by CLUSA; and the other, a three-country review of healthcare mutuals in Mali, Burkina Faso, and Benin, in which outside organizations pushed unsustainable local health insurance mutuals that failed to address the health issues of most local residents.

The Kenyan model was very different from these other two. The key was genuine community involvement in identifying local healthcare priorities and implementing actions that addressed them. A series of projects were initiated by CLUSA over more than a decade beginning in 2001. Toward the end of the project, more than 2,000 villages with a total estimated population of about 1 million had formed village and multi-village health committees.[103]

Altogether, I visited about 20 villages in different parts of the country, and conducted interviews and focus groups with well over 100 project staff, volunteer community health workers, and villagers.

Although villages participating in the CLUSA projects produced a wide variety of health and sanitation improvements at a very low cost per village, the program did not continue after 2012 because it didn't receive additional funding from USAID or financial support from the Kenyan government. Two key reasons for this were a major reduction of health funding in Kenya by USAID, and the fact that CLUSA was not eligible for direct health-related funding from USAID because it didn't meet the criterion of being a "Health NGO." It got its financial support by being a subcontractor to qualifying health NGOs, and thus was at the mercy of these NGOs for continued operation of its village health organizing.

Development lessons

A healthcare organizing approach that genuinely involves the active participation of community residents in identifying and solving their own health care problems works!

At relatively low cost, thousands of villages can be mobilized and establish ongoing community health initiatives that address a wide range of health-related issues.

This type of approach could be adapted to rural and urban communities in developing countries around the world and have a huge impact on the health and empowerment of local residents.

However, for village health initiatives to be successful in the long run, they need to be incorporated into a country's formal health delivery structure and receive ongoing financial support.

Because CLUSA was not defined as a health NGO, USAID did not allocate funds directly to the organization, but rather through primary contractors. This limited CLUSA's ability to make decisions about its own development strategy and weakened its control over its current and future funding.

Despite this constraint, CLUSA was able to provide an excellent organizing structure for village and multi-village health activities. But, as an NGO, it was not in a position to be able to provide continuing support after its funding ended.

Chapter 17

Reviewing a National Dairy Co-op System in Uganda – 2006

My assignment in Uganda was more of a case study than an evaluation. My job was to present the history of a dairy project carried out by Land O'Lakes[104] rather than to assess it and make recommendations.

What I discovered was a very impressive, integrated approach to dairy co-op development and marketing carried out over approximately a 10-year period. This was my first of several assignments consulting on Land O'Lakes' approach to dairy co-op development.

The basic approach goes something like this. Identify a group of rural communities in which there are a number of smallholder farmers who raise cattle. Organize village or other small group-based clusters of these farmers into primary co-ops. Work with the farmers to augment their animal husbandry skills and the quality and volume of the milk their cows produce. Establish a collection point for milk at the village or small group level that includes basic testing and recording of how much milk each farmer brings to the collection point. Aggregate the milk from each of the collection points at a secondary co-op where it is kept in a cooler until it is brought to a dairy processing facility.

In the case of Uganda, the project went well beyond this basic approach. Land O'Lakes developed a number of secondary co-ops serving groups of farmers in different parts of the country. These were connected at a tertiary level to further strengthen dairy production and marketing. Land O'Lakes worked with the co-ops on promoting the consumption of dairy products at the national level through advertising, event sponsorship, and other means. In many ways, this expanded approach approximates the kind of sophisticated dairy promotion that Land O'Lakes uses back in the United States. What's more, it worked!

As my report showed, Land O'Lakes gradually built up this bottom-to-top strategy during its decade-long development work in Uganda. But, it wasn't easy. One major obstacle was the short-term nature of much of its project funding from USAID. The developer had to negotiate more than five contract renewals with USAID over that ten-year period, several of which were not approved until the last minute. This meant that on a number of occasions, staff had to be prepared to close down the project on short notice. It is hard to do long-term planning in this kind of funding environment.

The second problem was that in the early years of the project, the largest dairy processing company in the country was government-owned, and not very responsive to the needs of small-scale dairy producers. Then things got worse. The state-owned dairy facility was sold to a private company that was even less responsive to dairy farmers.

Despite these major obstacles, the dairy co-ops were able to increase their market share in the country. After my brief sojourn in Uganda, the co-ops initiated an effort to establish a dairy co-op-owned processing facility to reduce their dependency on the large private company and a number of smaller processors in the country. My understanding is that this co-op-owned processing facility has not gotten off the ground.[105]

. . . .

Development lessons

The Land O'Lakes project in Uganda provides a valuable case study in how to develop co-ops, beginning at the grassroots level and extending all the way to a national program.

A key component for such a project is long-term funding.

The project also encountered obstacles that interfered with its success, including:

- The difficulty of carrying out a long-term project with a series of short-term contracts.
- Problems of unfair marketing relationships both with state-owned and privately-owned buyers.

Chapter 18

An Attempt to Develop a Livestock Cooperative in South Sudan – 2008

My primary assignment in South Sudan was to provide advice and assistance to the formation of a cooperative of semi-nomadic cattle and sheep herders. This was the most unusual of all my international consulting projects because the herders and their families were, for the most part, isolated from modern society, and were practicing a way of life that they had been for hundreds of years. For example, many of the villagers still wore animal skin clothing.

One new acquisition was AK-47s. A generations-old tradition of the young men was to carry out cattle raids on other groups of herders. This was a coming-of-age ritual in several ways: the raids were proof of bravery and manhood, and, if successful, provided the raiders with cattle that could be used to pay bride prices. Unfortunately, over the past several decades, machine guns had replaced spears as the weapons of choice, making these incursions far more deadly than they used to be.

Pre-teen boys, who predominated as herders around the village, sometimes sported these guns as a defense against raiders from other villages and tribes.

Despite the limited involvement of the herders in the broader society and economy, they saw the value in cooperatively marketing some of their cattle and sheep to the outside world in order to be able to purchase household goods, food, transistor radios, cell phones, and other items.

Even though a cooperative had not yet been formally organized when I arrived in the village, the Land O'Lakes staff had already set the stage for its formation. They had held several preparatory meetings with village leaders and villagers, and had constructed a large holding pen where cattle could be aggregated before they were shipped out and sold. The pen even included a solar-powered pump that provided water for the animals.

I attended a village-wide meeting where the next steps in forming the cooperative were discussed. The atmosphere was very positive and enthusiastic. I also met with staff members to strategize the final steps in forming the co-op. Everyone seemed excited about the prospect. There had not been a co-op incorporated in southern Sudan in more than 25 years. In large part this was because of an ongoing civil war between the south Sudanese and the government of Sudan.

But when I was there in 2008, a truce was in effect and the residents of South Sudan were scheduled to have a vote on independence in 2011. (South Sudan did become independent in 2011.) Thus, the timing was right to initiate economic development projects, including the start-up and reinvigoration of co-ops.

Shortly after I left South Sudan, I wrote out a detailed strategic paper for Land O'Lakes staff, recommending a step-by-step approach to formalizing the co-op. But, those steps were never taken, because USAID staff in Sudan abruptly terminated the project. This occurred, not because of any problems that the project was experiencing, but because of the arbitrary decision of USAID staff to locate a development project closer to the future border between Sudan and South Sudan.

So, Land O'Lakes staff had to shut down the project and leave the country with their work unfinished, and the intended members of the nascent co-op were left hanging. Since then, to my knowledge, the co-op never went into operation.

. . . .

Development lessons

The co-op business model can be applied in a wide variety of settings, even among people who are mostly isolated from the larger society and market economy.

In some cases, there are serious social, cultural, and even military issues that have to be addressed in order to create a compatible environment for co-op formation and other types of economic development.

Sometimes, funders play the perverse role of undercutting the very development projects they fund.

Chapter 19

Strategic Planning for a Cocoa Co-op in Madagascar – 2008

There were two big problems with my consulting assignment in Madagascar: the indifference of Chemonics, a large international development firm, which was the prime contractor for a major agricultural project in the country, of which my assignment was a small part; and my limited French-speaking skills.

As we saw in the case of the village health initiative in Kenya, the relationship between prime contractors and subcontractors can be problematic. In Madagascar, Land O'Lakes was a subcontractor to Chemonics, with the role of organizing co-ops as part of the larger agricultural project. So, my consulting contract was with Land O'Lakes, but ultimately, I was accountable to the head of the Chemonics project in Madagascar, who did not appear to have any interest in the cocoa farming co-op that I was there to work on.

If the marathon health mutual evaluation in Mali, Burkina Faso, and Benin was the most arduous international consulting project I've ever done, the cocoa project in Madagascar was the most stressful. The reason for the stress was that I had to communicate in French almost the entire time I was in the country.

When I had contracted with Land O'Lakes to do the project, part of the agreement was that I would have a translator working alongside me. It turned out that my "translator" spoke almost no English, and, as a result, I was forced to rely on my limited conversational French when I was in the field with my Malagasy colleagues, interviewing cocoa farmers, participating in meetings, and making presentations about strategies for organizing cocoa farmers into co-ops.

Despite the serious communication problems, I was able to prepare a co-op development strategy report (in English) that presented a very promising way for Malagasy cocoa farmers to form co-ops as part of an export marketing strategy. However, to my knowledge, Chemonics never implemented my proposed co-op development and marketing strategy.

. . . .

Development lessons
Beware of development organizations that go through the motions, but are not committed to following through on a co-op project.

Make sure that one's (or one's translator's) language skills fit the context of a project.

Chapter 20

Small-scale Commercial Farming in South Africa – 2008-2017

I made several visits to South Africa between 2008 and 2017, carrying out a variety of different tasks: conducting training sessions on cooperative development; doing case-study research on co-ops and potential co-ops in the country; identifying potential sources of funding for agricultural co-op development; and presenting a paper on co-op to co-op trade at an international cooperative gathering in Cape Town.

I enjoyed traveling around South Africa and getting a sense of the country, but, in terms of my co-op development efforts, I came away deeply frustrated, for a variety of reasons. For starters, South Africa has the highest level of income inequality of any country in the world. Most of the people suffering the brunt of this inequality are rural, Black subsistence or subsistence-plus farmers, under- and unemployed Blacks, and their families. Many of the smallholder farmers have the potential to become small-scale commercial farmers, but receive very little development assistance to help make the transition. Instead, in a continuation of the practices of apartheid, commercial agriculture is dominated by large-scale white farmers.

It is worth noting that most of the commercial agriculture in sub-Saharan Africa is by smallholder farmers. For example, Kenya has built a strong agricultural economy mostly based on small-farm production. An additional effect of a smallholder agricultural system is to slow the migration of rural residents to urban areas, thus reducing overcrowding and poor living conditions in the cities.

Ever since the end of apartheid and the beginning of democratic elections in 1994, the national government, dominated by the African National Congress, has promised to redistribute farmland in order to increase Black ownership. These redistribution efforts have had very limited success.[106]

Research project on smallholder farming in South Africa

My last foray into this apartheid-like agricultural economy was in 2017 when Mpumelelo Ncwadi, a South African colleague, and I visited about 20 farms and co-ops and conducted interviews to determine possible ways in which smallholder Black farmers could become more involved in commercial agriculture.

We were affiliated with the University of Wisconsin's Center for Integrated Agricultural Systems, and the University of Fort Hare, Eastern Cape, South Africa, when we carried out this research.

We identified three promising approaches to increase commercial Black farming:

- **Medium- and large-scale Black family farms** had had limited commercial success to date, but showed promise for the future, especially if the farmers were members of multipurpose cooperatives.

- **Smallholder Black commercial farms** had very good potential, if they received coordinated assistance through co-ops or similar programs.

- **Small-scale livestock owners** also showed high potential for commercial success if they participated in co-ops or other coordinated programs involving rotational grazing, access to credit, breeding support, and marketing assistance.[107]

We shared our paper with a number of agricultural organizations, government agencies, and others, but have not yet seen any improvements in this terribly unjust situation.

. . . .

Development lessons

There is a litany of changes that need to be made in order to bring about significant involvement of smallholder farmers in South African commercial agriculture:

- Reduce the near-monopoly of large white farmers in commercial agriculture.

- Launch effective initiatives by the national and provincial governments to increase the number of Black, smallholder commercial farms

- Provide domestic and/or international funding and technical assistance for innovative approaches to address the current inequitable situation.

- Secure commitments by wholesale and retail buyers to enter into purchasing contracts with smallholder groups.

Chapter 21

Analysis of a Village Development Program in Kenya – 2008

This was an unusual international assignment for me because it involved community development rather than co-op development.

The Aga Khan Foundation is a well-respected charitable and development organization based in Switzerland.[108] Most of its assistance is targeted to Muslim communities around the world. The foundation had been carrying out a long-term project in a number of villages on the eastern side of Kenya in the Mombasa area.

My job was to evaluate the village-level activities of the foundation. There was another, somewhat hidden, agenda as well. The foundation wanted to move away from this village development model, and was looking for evidence that the current approach wasn't working very well.

That second agenda item created a problem because my site visits and interviews indicated that the foundation's village development approach was generally successful. That's what I wrote in my report, but that's not what the staff wanted to hear. The review process for my report was truly mind-boggling. I received a set of edits and comments from five or more staff members that were almost as long as the report itself. That's a bit of an exaggeration, but I've never before or since been hammered with such a lengthy critique of a project report. Because staff had a preconceived expectation of receiving a negative report, they reacted by micro-questioning my mostly positive evaluation.

I reacted by figuratively throwing my hands up in the air and saying "I give up." When I did that, they backed off on asking me to respond to their highly detailed comments and questions, and requested a less daunting revision of the report, which I provided and they accepted.

....

Development lessons

Completing this assignment for the Aga Khan Foundation was an unpleasant experience. The research itself was interesting and educational, and exposed me to an effective community development model.

The problem was that the foundation staff didn't want a positive evaluation of the program, and they took it out on the messenger – me -- when they didn't hear what they wanted to hear.

This project touches on a number of issues:

- Problems resulting when organizational representatives have preconceived expectations about a project's performance and are not open to hearing something different.

- Internal review processes characterized by micro-management and bias.

- Too many cooks in the kitchen.

Chapter 22

Developing and Monitoring Dairy Co-ops in Sri Lanka – 2009-2011

As in South Sudan, I worked in Sri Lanka shortly after a civil war. In the Sri Lankan case, the war was between the government and a Tamil rebel organization. The war lasted from 1983 to 2009.

I worked on contract with Land O'Lakes, primarily in Batticaloa, a Tamil village on the eastern coast of the country, in 2009 and 2011. My job was to help develop and monitor progress on the formation of a multi-tiered dairy cooperative.

Many of the villagers around Batticaloa raised cattle for milk and meat, but were mostly not focused on getting products to market. Land O'Lakes was implementing a dairy co-op project intended to generate revenue for these small-scale farmers by aggregating milk from clusters of farmers, and shipping it on to a commercial dairy for processing and marketing. The model was similar to the one that Land O'Lakes used in Uganda. Primary co-ops were organized among neighboring farmers, who brought their milk to nearby collection points for weighing and testing. The milk from these collection points was then brought to a secondary co-op location where it was kept in coolers and then delivered to the dairy processing plant.

This was a cost-effective way to get small farmers into the market economy, and for them to get a decent return on the milk produced by their cows.

When I returned for my second visit in 2011, most of the co-ops were up and running and doing well. But there was one issue in particular that presaged future problems. The privately-owned dairy company that collected and processed the milk didn't appear to like the fact that it was purchasing milk through a group of co-operatives rather than directly from the dairy farmers. In one interview I had with a company executive, he basically stated that he'd rather have the company deal directly with individual farmers to avoid having to negotiate with the co-ops. This attitude did not bode well for the future relationship between the company and the network of co-ops.

. . . .

Development lessons

The Batticaloa project is another example of the effectiveness of the Land O'Lakes dairy co-op development model based on milk collection at local primary co-ops, aggregation at the secondary co-op level, and delivery to, and processing by, one or more dairy processors.

As in Uganda, relying on a state or private dairy processor can create tension between farmers and processors, because the latter has a tendency to want to drive down prices they pay for milk. But, since the farmers are organized in co-ops, the processors are not easily able to do so.

The fact that the farmers of Batticaloa were primarily members of the Tamil minority ethnic group, and the owners of the dairy company were Sinhalese – the majority ethnic group in the country – probably added to this tension.

Chapter 23

Launching a Co-op Development Campaign in Bhutan – 2010

Doing a three-week consulting assignment in Bhutan was an unusual, exotic, and frustrating experience. The country of less than 1 million inhabitants is situated on the border between China and India, with Himalayan mountain peaks ranging up to 23,000 feet (7,000 m) on the Chinese side and subtropical lowlands on the Indian side. It is very probably the "steepest" country in the world. Its mountainous topography and plethora of beautiful Buddhist monasteries and shrines make it a very popular attraction for tourists, even though the government limits access by requiring them to spend a hefty amount of money per day while they are in the country.

As a consultant to the government, I got to enjoy Bhutan's beauty without having to pay this cost. I spent most of my time in the capital, Thimphu, which is about a mile and a half (2,300 m) above sea level. My job was to advise the Department of Cooperatives on how to implement the country's relatively new cooperative law.

Another fascinating thing about Bhutan was that it was undergoing a transition from an autocratic kingdom to a democratic constitutional monarchy. The kingdom of Bhutan began in the early 1600s. In 1999, the king decreed that the country would become a parliamentary democracy with a titular royal family (a model similar to the United Kingdom) beginning with the ascension of his son to the throne. The constitution was enacted in 2008. So, my assignment was in the youngest democracy in the world.

The frustrating part of my job was providing advice on cooperative development to an audience that wanted to move at a glacially slow pace, despite the opportunities for rapid co-op growth. Surprisingly to me, the go-slow advocates were primarily composed of expatriate advisers to the co-op department. The head of the department was far more sympathetic to a more assertive approach. Since I was a short-term consultant and my cautious opponents were long-term advisors, I was destined to lose the battle.

To provide a sense of the slow-motion bureaucracy in the Bhutanese government, the co-op law that was about to be implemented had been passed in 2000, but did not have accompanying regulations developed until 2010 – a ten-year lag between enactment and rules for implementation.

The main reason that I saw an opportunity to get a fast start on co-op development, now that the long-delayed regulations were in place, was because Bhutan had organized several hundred well-established forestry and farm associations, many of which were ripe to switch to cooperative businesses. In fact, I spent part of my time in the country doing site visits to these farm and forestry organizations to validate their readiness to become co-ops. I wasn't alone in my belief about co-op conversion. Many of the Bhutanese government advisers to these organizations agreed. I calculated that 50 to 100 of them could become co-ops during an initial two-year period.

In my final report, I laid out a step-by-step approach to converting these entities into co-ops, including draft forms that could be filled out to help facilitate the transition. This was all to no avail, because the go-slow bureaucrats were adamant in their preferences for establishing a handful of co-ops in the first couple of years rather than having a more assertive co-op development campaign. The final score: Bureaucrats: 1, EG: 0.

So, the best part of my trip to Bhutan was spent visiting Buddhist monasteries, hiking, and enjoying the breathtaking scenery. My co-op development assignment was a bust, at least in the short-term. Otherwise, I had a wonderful trip.

. . . .

Development lessons
The big lesson here is that bureaucratic inertia can be a huge impediment to cooperative development. (That was also the case in Ghana, where an attempt by the CLUSA co-op team and a host of Ghanaian cooperators was not able to convince the government to replace an outdated, colonially based, co-op law. This case study is presented in Chapter 32.)

A difference between the two examples, however, is the role in Bhutan played by expatriate advisers in holding back co-op development.

Chapter 24

Case Study of an Agroforestry Project in Niger – 2011

My evaluation of the Moringa project in Niger as a CLUSA consultant was probably the most educationally rewarding and hopeful of my international consulting assignments.

Niger is one of the poorest countries in the world as measured by GDP per person. Most of the country is occupied by the Sahara Desert, and most of the rest is in the Sahel region of northern Africa characterized by low rainfall and low-productivity soils.

Around the time I was there, Boko Haram extremists based in northern Nigeria occasionally raided Niger from the south, and ISIS and other terrorist groups dropped down from the desert from time to time to cause trouble, including kidnapping Westerners. So, I was almost always accompanied by one or more colleagues from Niger. When I was alone, I was cautioned to stay within a prescribed area near my hotel.

Given these negative factors, why was my trip to Niger such a positive experience? One important reason was that the project director, Zakaria Mamoudou, and I got along very well. He was my guide and interpreter during most of my stay in the country. The second key reason was the success of the Moringa project, and the positive effects that it was having on the people whom I met, and more broadly on the health, nutrition, and economy of Niger.

So, what is Moringa and why was its proliferation a big deal? Moringa is classified as a kind of tree. But, it's a very special tree. Among other attributes, it tolerates semi-arid climate conditions, grows quickly when watered regularly, produces highly nutritious leaves that can be harvested monthly throughout the year, and is a popular ingredient in local dishes. The leaves can also be pulverized into a powder and mixed with milk and other foods, especially as a nutritional supplement for kids. Because many Nigerois suffer from periodic undernutrition, Moringa is an excellent addition to the food supply.

The purpose of the project was to distribute newly developed Moringa hybrid seeds throughout the country, assist farmers to cultivate the resulting trees properly, and produce enough leaves, not only for family and local consumption, but for marketing into the urban areas of the country. As production increased, co-ops were seen as a key means to aggregate, dry, and sell the leaves on behalf of member farmers.

Based on my visits to a couple of dozen rural and urban sites around Niger, the project was going gangbusters. Thousands of farmers and gardeners were growing the trees successfully, and consuming and marketing dried leaves and powder. They were being sold by market women in cities and large villages in many locations throughout the country. And this had all been accomplished in about three years.

The missing piece was cooperative marketing. Because production was still ramping up, I was told by project team members and farmers that additional volume was required before co-ops needed to come into play in order to formalize and expand the marketing initiative.

Even with the nascent co-op component, I was impressed by the other aspects of the project, and presented a very positive evaluation in my final report. I recently received an email from Mamoudou, confirming that the distribution of Moringa leaves across the country continued to go well, although there didn't appear to be much co-op marketing of this product.

Development lessons

The project was an example of a successful initiative to improve nutrition and generate economic benefits rapidly and on a fairly large scale. Several things created this success: a new Moringa hybrid with several desirable attributes – faster-growing trees and larger leaves; good taste and high nutritional value; a well-organized CLUSA project team with an effective dissemination plan; and funding from USAID.

When I left Niger, it was too early to tell if the co-op component would take shape as planned. In fact, there is reason to doubt that it would because of the imminent completion of the project. But even without the formation of marketing co-ops, I consider the project a success because Moringa was being produced and marketed effectively by individual farmers and informal groups of farmers, by middlemen and women, and by urban and village market women. I would have preferred the involvement of co-ops in order to provide a larger share of the retail sales price back to the farmers, but there were plenty of benefits even without the higher return.

Chapter 25

Evaluation of a Soybean Project in Mozambique – 2012

In 2012, the year following my assignment in Niger, I conducted a somewhat similar evaluation for CLUSA in Mozambique, a final review of a five-year project in which about 5,000 smallholder farmers were introduced to the cultivation and marketing of non-GMO soybeans. "Non-GMO" means that these beans were not genetically modified. Many countries, in Europe and elsewhere, don't allow the importation of feed or food containing GMOs.

There is an interesting backstory to this project. Felleskjøpet, a large Norwegian agricultural cooperative, had been looking for a way to import non-GMO soybeans because the climate of Norway is not conducive to soybean production. The co-op identified the area around Gurue in north central Mozambique as well-suited for this production. The co-op and the Norwegian Agency for Development Cooperation contracted with CLUSA to run the project because of its long history of providing co-op development assistance in Mozambique. These are the origins of the project I was hired to evaluate.

I took a five-hour trip by Land Rover from Nampula, a large city in northern Mozambique, to Gurue. Since there was not much tourism in this area, lodging for travelers was scarce. I stayed in a room in the rectory of a local Catholic church, and had most of my meals with the priests and brothers there.

My work consisted of visiting farms that were part of the project, interviewing farmers and project staff, combing through five years of project reports and other data, and preparing an evaluation of my findings. What I found was a multi-part story:

1. The project had done an excellent job of training and distributing inputs to more than 5,000 smallholder farmers, providing technical assistance as they grew their soy crops, and helping to find market outlets for the soybeans produced. The project also had a major literacy component and an emphasis on training women farmers. Both of these aspects of the project also went very well.

2. In terms of co-op development, however, there wasn't much going on. Due, in part, to a lack of emphasis by project staff, farmers were not ready to effectively operate primary co-ops, where seeds and other inputs could be distributed, and where harvested soybeans could be aggregated and stored. Secondary

co-ops, responsible for the delivery of inputs to, and the marketing of beans from the primary co-ops, were even less developed.

So, I gave strong positive grades to the agriculture, literacy, and gender components of the project, and a low grade to the cooperative development part.

I concluded that, in general, project staff did not prioritize co-op development. Why not – especially since CLUSA specializes in co-op development, and one of the main funders for the project was a co-op? Although I didn't put this explicitly in the report, I attributed the lack of emphasis on co-ops to the biases of the in-country project leadership (the country director in Nampula, and the succession of on-site project directors in Gurue). Co-op development did not appear to be a priority to them. As one project director said to me, "You can't organize Mozambican farmers into co-ops." This sounded like a stereotype and a self-fulfilling prophecy. Several Mozambican project staff members concurred with me in this assessment.

Despite these problems on the co-op side, I considered the GMO soybean project a success. A large number of subsistence and subsistence-plus farmers had become profitable, small-scale commercial farmers. Even without the supportive role that co-ops would have played, the farmers were able to get inputs and find markets anyway, although probably not as economically as they would have been able to through well-organized co-ops.

A major irony of this project was that the Norwegian co-op, that had played key roles in initiating and funding the project, did not receive any of the soybeans produced by it. The reason for this was that the poultry industry in Mozambique was growing rapidly at the same time as the farmers in the project were increasing their production of soybeans. Since soy is an excellent source of protein for poultry, almost all of the soy production from the project went to the Mozambican poultry industry, leaving the Norwegian co-op high and dry.

The Norwegians were delighted with the success of the project anyway, so delighted that they and the Norwegian government funded two additional five-year phases of the project that were much larger than the original phase. About 30,000 farmers were trained in the second phase, and about the same number of farmers are included in the third phase which ends in 2022.

In addition to all of the components of the first phase, the additional phases emphasize rotational farming and conservation agriculture, which "increases productivity (40-60%), decreases agricultural losses, and mitigates the negative impact of climate change by developing the economic and environmental resilience of farmers.[109]

By the way, the Norwegian co-op ended up securing most of its non-GMO soybeans from Brazil instead of Mozambique.

. . . .

Development lessons
Some of the lessons from this project are similar to those from the Moringa project in Niger.

- The projects were very successful in ramping up agricultural production among male and female smallholder farmers.

- Both had strong domestic markets for their products.

- The level of success of both projects generated follow-up projects.

- Neither accomplished much in the way of cooperative development.

- A major difference was that there appeared to be neglect of co-ops in Mozambique, and more of a timing problem in Niger. That is, the growth of Moringa leaf marketing had not yet reached the point of benefiting strongly from co-op purchasing and marketing by the time the project was ending.

• Another difference was the role of literacy training in the Mozambican project.

• A final difference was the emphasis on conservation agriculture in Mozambique.

Chapter 26

Designing an Integrated Cooperative Project in Haiti – 2013

Working with staff from the World Council of Credit Unions (WOCCU), HealthPartners, and CLUSA, I participated in exploring the development of an integrated agricultural, credit union, and health project in Haiti.

The idea behind the exploratory phase was to design a co-op development project or set of projects in Haiti in which three US NGOs – CLUSA, WOCCU, and Health Partners – would coordinate their work with development organizations in Haiti. All three organizations had very good track records in co-op development. CLUSA had almost 70 years of experience in developing agriculture-related co-ops, healthcare projects, and other initiatives. WOCCU had developed and assisted financial co-ops in dozens of countries around the world. HealthPartners was a very successful health cooperative in Minnesota, and had done pioneering healthcare work in Uganda. CLUSA and WOCCU were already engaged in projects in Haiti.

My participation in the project consisted primarily of being the surrogate representative from CLUSA at two meetings in Haiti with representatives from the other two U.S. organizations and 10 or so Haitian NGOs and international organizations working in Haiti.

Several things bothered me from the beginning. There was no clear idea among the three U.S. NGOs of what a joint project might look like. The trips to Haiti had more the feel of fishing expeditions than project-development meetings. I felt particularly uncomfortable about taking up the time of, and creating expectations among, the Haiti-based people at the table. A number of very good ideas were presented, but the U.S. folks didn't yet have the funds to follow up on them. They were betting on the "come" – that is, that they would be able to get follow-up money from USAID to carry out the joint projects discussed. To my knowledge, no such funds ever materialized. As a result, the main effects of the project were to create false expectations among the participating organizations and, possibly, to poison the well for future collaboration and trust.

. . . .

Development lessons

The primary lesson that I derived from this exploratory project was the importance of having a clear plan of action and some funding to back it up before engaging with potential partners. If the meetings in Haiti had been billed as part of a research project to identify potential co-op-related initiatives, that would have been a more legitimate approach. But that wasn't what was done. The impression given was that the meetings were a prelude to one or more joint development projects, even though the money had not been secured (or even tentatively promised) to fund such projects.

Chapter 27

The Development of Producer Co-ops in Indonesia and East Timor

The longest-lasting international cooperative development initiative in the world is taking place in Indonesia and East Timor. CLUSA began working in Indonesia in 1977. Forty-three years later, it's still there – and in East Timor, which became independent from Indonesia in 2002. CLUSA continues to carry out a range of co-op development and support projects involving shrimp, fish, vanilla beans, furniture, mushrooms, cocoa, organic and specialty coffee, cinnamon and other spices, baby corn and other items.[110]

I interviewed several people knowledgeable about CLUSA's long-term work in Indonesia and East Timor as part of a report on co-op to co-op trade that I prepared for the U.S. Overseas Cooperative Development Council in 2013, and followed up with further research in 2020. I would love to visit this project, but have not had the opportunity to date.

In East Timor, CLUSA played a major role in organizing, and continues to provide support services to Cooperativa Café Timor. This is the country's largest farmer cooperative – with about 30,000 members – and one of the largest single-source suppliers of certified organic coffee in the world.[111]

A demand-driven strategy is a key aspect of CLUSA's success in developing export-oriented cooperatives in these countries. It doesn't just assist co-ops to produce products, it targets products to already-identified markets. In addition, the project has emphasized adding value to commodity products, primarily via joint ventures, in which co-ops partner with other businesses to secure capital, expertise, and international trade connections. These business partners include Cooperative Business International (CBI), which originally was organized by NCBA in 1994 and then reorganized as a privately-owned company in the late 1990s, with NCBA as a minority owner.

. . . .

Development lessons

This example illustrates that the three- to five-year duration of many cooperative development projects often grossly underestimates the time required to launch a successful cooperative project, and to meet the long-term assistance needs of co-ops in developing countries.

The example also emphasizes the importance of market-driven cooperative development and the successful use of joint ventures to add value to products.

Chapter 28

Key Lessons from These International Projects

Why are international cooperative development projects successful, partially successful, or failures? This chapter provides a comparative analysis of key reasons for success and failure, and makes suggestions for improving development projects in the future.

The international cooperative development projects reviewed above have produced mixed results. My favorites are the community health initiative in Kenya, the comprehensive dairy project in Uganda, the Moringa project in Niger, the soybean project in

Mozambique, and the long-term CLUSA project in Indonesia and East Timor.

Sometimes development organizations are primarily responsible for a project's success or failure. In other cases, the funder deserves most of the credit or blame. There are also cases in which the government of the host country or local leaders make or break a project. And then there are projects that succeed or fail for multiple reasons.

Development organizations

Overall, I was impressed with the dedication and quality of work by the staff members of co-op development organizations that I encountered during the past 20 years. One criticism that I have is that in some cases, there was not enough emphasis on the "co-op" part of development. This was partly a function of the short timeframe in which many of the projects had to operate. For example, it was easier to accomplish the delivery of agricultural and health assistance than it was to help local residents create well-functioning co-ops.

During the course of my international development work, I occasionally encountered approaches to development, including "cooperative" development, that were ill-conceived and not in the best interests of the recipients of the assistance. One example is a "flavor of the day" approach to development, often resulting from a for-profit developer convincing a funder, e.g. USAID, that it had a unique approach to community health care, small business development, or some other development niche, that would work wonders for solving local problems. Developers who play this game well push several flavors at the same time, and then move on to new flavors when the old ones don't pan out as promised. Some funders don't catch on to this scheme, or choose not to penalize developers for the many flavors that fail and are jettisoned along the way. I would put some of the health mutual projects in

West Africa and Chemonics' cocoa project in Madagascar in this category.

Development funders

USAID and other development-related organizations often set different project priorities for different countries without clear rationales. For example, during at least the past decade, the USAID office in South Africa has given a low priority to assisting small-holder Black farmers to increase their involvement in commercial agriculture. This decision has been despite the fact that South Africa has the most unequal distribution of income of any country in the world, and rural Black South Africans are the poorest residents of the country. For some reason, perhaps because South Africa has a relatively large gross domestic product (which is really no reason at all), USAID has shown no interest in assisting the country's poor Black rural residents.

Sometimes, development decisions are made at the whim of the local USAID office or other development organization staff. For example, in the South Sudan co-op development project I assisted, the USAID country director arbitrarily closed down the project despite the fact that it was progressing well, and transferred the funds to a project in another part of the country, leaving the previous project without any assistance at a critical point in its development.

Host countries

There are two examples in particular among the 25 or so projects in which I participated that the host country was a key player in making the project less successful than it could have been. One was Ghana, in which the national government resisted, rather than supported, a reform of the national cooperative law that would have created a genuinely democratic context for cooperatives in the country. The other was Bhutan, where the national department of cooperatives took an overly cautious approach to implementing its cooperative law. This resulted in a much-more timid introduction of co-ops to the country than was necessary.

. . . .

Development lessons

In comparing the international co-op case studies presented above, there are a wide variety of reasons for the degree of success or failure of the projects reviewed. In a few cases, the funder or the host country played a decisive role in undercutting the projects. For the most part, however, the co-op development organization itself was primarily responsible for the project's outcome. Most of those out-comes were good, although ironically, the co-op part of the develop-ment process was sometimes the weakest link. The short duration of many of the projects was a key factor responsible for inadequately developed co-ops.

CLUSA's long-term, multi-faceted project in Indonesia and East Timor, and the decade-long dairy project of Land O'Lakes in Uganda, are examples of successful co-op development, in large part because the organizations had both the expertise and the time to assist in the building of these co-ops.

Strengthening the Building Blocks of the Cooperative Community

The previous two sections of the book have focused on the historical development of seven cooperative sectors and on the history of cooperative development itself, and also on 18 recent examples of international cooperative development projects. I have drawn lessons and provided comparative analyses to better understand the cases presented, and to contribute to improving cooperative development efforts in the future.

This section looks at seven cooperative "building blocks" – key factors that influence the success or failure of co-op development projects. This section also makes a set of recommendations for strengthening and better coordinating these building blocks during the next decade – and for the remainder of the 21st-century.

What are these building blocks? The seven factors that I write about below are: cooperative entrepreneurship, research, education, technical and organizational support, laws and regulations, finance, and cooperation among cooperatives, plus the integration of these building blocks.

Following are two brief examples of the use of these building blocks in different cooperative sectors.

- As described in Chapter 1, mutual insurance companies were initially formed by local groups of business owners and other citizens who developed ways to mobilize community members to fight fires quickly and to pool funds in order to rebuild after fires. When new mutuals formed, they followed these early models, supplemented with advice from established mutuals.

Interestingly, in the United States, laws and regulations related to these mutuals were not developed until several decades after this co-op sector came into being.

- Electric co-ops in the United States were formed in rural communities to fill gaps left by for-profit utilities. Initially, these co-ops were slow to develop because of the high cost of generating electricity and transmitting it over long distances. A key factor that accelerated their development was the passage of the Rural Electrification Act in 1936, which provided low-cost loans to electric utilities in rural areas. Once this missing financial piece had been filled, there was rapid growth of rural electric co-ops across the United States.

Both of these examples illustrate the use of cooperative building blocks in launching and expanding new cooperative sectors. It is important to recognize that in different sectors, the importance of each of the building blocks may vary substantially. For example, mutual insurance was financed by pooling funds of mutual members. In the case of rural electric co-ops, covering the high start-up costs was made possible by a federal loan program. These two co-op sectors also differ substantially in the way they were replicated and adapted. In the early years of mutuals, neighborhoods and communities learned from the examples of other mutuals as guides to their formation. Rural electrics also benefited from lessons learned from other co-ops, but were also very strongly affected by the need to conform to the requirements for receiving federal approval for their loan financing.

The following chapters provide information on each of the building blocks and make recommendations for using them more effectively to strengthen the cooperative community between 2021 and 2030.

Chapter 29

Cooperative Entrepreneurship

The online Business Dictionary defines entrepreneurship as, "The capacity and willingness to develop, organize and manage a business venture along with any of its risks in order to make a profit."[112]

Cooperative entrepreneurship differs in one important way from this definition in that the priority goal is to provide a service rather than to make a profit. That isn't to say that profits are not important, but rather that they are secondary to the service mission of the organization. So, in the example of the rural electric co-ops mentioned above, the primary purpose is to provide reliable and affordable electricity to the member-owners of the co-ops. To do this, each co-op must generate a surplus in order to stay in business and continue to carry out its mission.

Cooperative entrepreneurs mentioned in the historical section of the book include Benjamin Franklin, the Rochdale Pioneers, Edward Filene, José María Arizmendiarrieta, and Rod Nilsestuen.

In international development, many of the cooperative entrepreneurs are organizations rather than individuals. For example, CLUSA, Land O'Lakes, the 10 organizational members of the Cooperatives Europe Development Platform,[113] and other international development organizations.

In addition to these co-op entrepreneurs, there are hundreds of thousands of individuals and small organizing groups who play lead roles in starting co-ops and in infusing new energy and direction into established co-ops.

The Mondragon Federation, discussed in Chapter 6, provides a unique example of cooperative entrepreneurship. Starting with one worker-owned business in the 1950s, this co-op federation expanded to include well over 200 businesses and other organizations. A key catalyst for this growth and diversification has been the research, development, and financing arms of the federation that prepare, oversee, and provide funding for the implementation of business plans. These R&D components also review business plans of Mondragon network members, and mentor new businesses to increase the likelihood of their success.

This co-op development approach at Mondragon is the inspiration for the first "building block" recommendation.

Coordinated support for cooperative entrepreneurship

RECOMMENDATION 1

Build on the work of the International Cooperative Entrepreneurship Think Tank (ICETT) to create a "hands-on" network of cooperative business planning centers.

These centers would help new and established co-ops and multi-co-op initiatives to develop and sustain innovative co-op businesses.

ICETT was established by the International Cooperative Alliance in 2018 "to serve as a strategic hub at the service of the cooperative movement to strengthen the entrepreneurial performance of cooperatives."[114].

Recommendation one is strongly supportive of ICETT, and encourages this new entity to coordinate direct entrepreneurial assistance to co-ops and groups of co-ops in addition to its think tank functions.

For example, the 17 Sustainable Development Goals (SDGs) established by the United Nations in 2015 include a rich array of cooperative entrepreneurial opportunities.[115] Co-ops are already carrying out some of these goals in renewable energy, community health, housing, and other areas. But some of these initiatives face problems of scale, efficiency, and coordination, and could greatly benefit from assistance provided by ICETT and other co-op entrepreneurial support organizations.

Regarding SDG 7 "providing energy for all," the co-op community has thus far been helping to create and expand energy co-ops for a small percentage of the almost 1 billion people without electricity.[116]

With the help of ICETT and similar initiatives, the co-op community could approach the UN energy goal in a much more comprehensive and efficient manner than it has thus far. A key element in a more ambitious approach would be the involvement of one or more cooperative business planning centers to research, design, and assist in the implementation of renewable energy cooperatives that would reach many millions of new energy co-op members in developing countries.

Similar potential applies to co-op involvement in other SDG goals. Cooperative entrepreneurship centers could plan and coordinate much more ambitious co-op development projects in order to contribute to the achievement of a number of SDGs. Some of these potential enterprises are presented in the cooperative opportunities section of the book presented below.

Cooperative entrepreneurship centers have a broad range of other applications as well. Just as Mondragon identifies cooperative business opportunities that create stable, well-paying jobs in the Basque region of Spain and in other domestic and international locations, these centers could also be used to identify job-creating co-ops in communities and regions with high unemployment rates, and to revitalize and restructure co-ops that have fallen on hard times.

The key point to emphasize about co-op entrepreneurship is that what is now a set of generally small-scale, disjointed efforts to expand co-op businesses and sectors could become much more coordinated and strategic initiatives.

Chapter 30

Cooperative Research

There are many ways that research strengthens the co-op community. A few examples are presented in this chapter.

Research as part of business planning

Cooperative entrepreneurship, discussed in Chapter 29, includes a number of research elements. A big part of putting together and implementing a successful business plan involves research – on technology, markets, financial viability, and other areas.

Historical research

One of my favorite examples of cooperative research is the two-volume history of cooperatives in the United States written by Joseph Knapp, and published in 1969 and 1973.[117] I relied heavily on Knapp's work in the historical section of this book. Within these two volumes, I was particularly impressed by his recounting of the rise of U.S. credit unions and the lessons from the organizing strategy that led to the creation of thousands of credit unions across the United States from the 1920s through the 1940s.

Knapp's work is an example of well-documented, historical research. This is just one of a range of research approaches that inform our understanding of the origins, growth strategies, and future potential of the cooperative community.

Data analysis

Each year since 2005, the International Cooperative Alliance (ICA) has been publishing data on the 300 largest cooperatives in the world. In 2012, ICA joined forces with Euricse (European

Research Institute on Cooperative and Social Enterprises) to provide expanded analyses on these co-ops in annual reports of the World Cooperative Monitor.[118] For those of us who are interested in contemporary trends in key international cooperative businesses and sectors, this is an invaluable resource.

This periodic, primarily quantitative report is quite different from Knapp's mostly qualitative, historical analysis of the cooperative community. They both provide a wealth of information useful to understanding the state of cooperatives in the world and guidance on recent and future trends.

A census of co-ops

As many of us in the cooperative community know, 2012 was the UN-designated International Year of Cooperatives. One side note to that very successful celebratory and educational year was some unspent funds donated by Rabobank, one of the largest cooperative banks in the world, to the UN Department of Economic and Social Affairs. The Department decided to allocate some of these funds to the preparation of an unprecedented worldwide census of cooperatives.[119]

Dave Grace and Associates was the research and consulting group selected to gather and present a report on the data. "Measuring the Size and Scope of the Cooperative Economy: Results of the 2014 Global Census on Co-operatives" was published in April 2014. It provided information on cooperatives, members, assets, annual gross revenue, and other co-op data for 145 countries, representing the large majority of co-ops in the world.[120] This 2014 report remains the only systematic effort to quantify information on cooperatives from all over the world.

Interactive data analysis

CoMetrics provides an excellent example of an interactive research tool for cooperatives. The technique was first developed for retail co-op members of National Co+op Grocers (NCG) in the United States. In this interactive approach, retail food co-ops report their financial data each quarter – and other related data on a less frequent basis. CoMetrics aggregates the information, conducts comparative analyses of the data from the participating co-ops, and sends these analyses back to all of the co-ops and to NCG, where the information is used to improve performance. This research application began in the 1990s as a pilot project with a small number of grocery co-ops. Now, all of NCG's member co-ops participate in this data-sharing program.[121]

In recent years, the CoMetrics methodology has been applied to additional co-op sectors and to groups of nonprofit organizations, and has excellent potential for expanded use.[122]

Problem-solving research

A sixth research example is a recent evaluation of a co-op development project being carried out by Self Help Africa in Ethiopia. The evaluation, coordinated by the U.S. Overseas Cooperative Development Council, had two very specific purposes: to determine why farmers were selling a large percentage of their malt barley to outside buyers rather than to their cooperatives; and to identify ways to increase malt barley sales to the co-ops. The researchers were able to identify a number of reasons for the "side-selling," and recommended new buying practices for the co-ops to reduce these sales.[123]

The malt barley research project is a very good example of applying qualitative and quantitative research skills to understand a specific problem faced by a co-op or group of co-ops, and to use that understanding to solve or ameliorate the problem.

Opportunities for improving cooperative research

Despite the diverse examples of international cooperative research presented above, there remain significant gaps in these types of research. The following recommendations are intended to fill some of these gaps.

Cooperative census

There is no periodic, comprehensive analysis of international data on cooperatives. The World Co-operative Monitor presents annual data on the 300 largest co-ops in the world and self-reported data from other co-ops. But the 2014 co-op census by Dave Grace and Associates is the only comprehensive data collection project on the international cooperative community. To my knowledge, there are no plans to follow up on this project.

RECOMMENDATION 2

Carry out a periodic international cooperative census.

The Committee for the Promotion and Advancement of Cooperatives (COPAC),[124] *the UN Department of Economic and Social Affairs,*[125] *or a similar international cooperative entity, should coordinate a periodic (e.g., every-five-year) worldwide census of cooperatives that collects information on a small number of major variables such as those in the World Cooperative Monitor and the 2014 Global Census of Cooperatives.*

Coopedia

Up until Coopedia was inaugurated in 2020, there had been no well-organized, comprehensive, frequently updated, virtual library of books, periodicals, and research papers on cooperatives.

RECOMMENDATION 3

Build on the work begun by Coopedia by broadening the information it contains and making it more accessible to users.

The Coopedia Knowledge Base is "a collaborative search engine listing resources (guides, articles, videos, books, and more) on cooperative entrepreneurship."[126] *It is a joint project of the International Cooperative Alliance (ICA) and the European Union.*

Coopedia is an excellent new resource for the co-op community, and for those interested in learning about co-ops and how to form them. One thing I noticed in reviewing the Coopedia site is that it could be designed in a more user-friendly manner. For example, unlike Wikipedia, one has to sign in to the site in order to use it and to specify the resource or topic that one wishes to search. These are intended as minor criticisms. My overall reaction is delight that the new resource is available.

Applied cooperative research

Although there is some strategic analysis related to the role of co-ops in addressing problems around the world, there is not enough specific research undertaken to address these problems. For example, the Alliance states that the UN's Strategic Development Goal Program and the implementation of measures to address climate change are priorities for the international co-op community, but it has not yet taken the lead in coordinating research and development in carrying out such cooperative initiatives. Recommendation 1 – Creating an international network of cooperative entrepreneurship centers – would go a long way to filling this gap.

There is also not nearly enough evaluative research done on co-ops and co-op development projects that provides guidance and lessons learned for the broader co-op community.

RECOMMENDATION 4
Form a consortium on applied cooperative research.

The purpose of the consortium would be to create an interactive relationship between applied researchers and cooperative development projects in which researchers would apply their skills to evaluate cooperative performance and to help solve specific co-op development problems.

The ICA already has a Committee on Cooperative Research (CCR), the primary activities of which are to organize cooperative research events and to publish papers from these events. One possibility would be to organize the consortium as a specific sub-part of CCR, and to coordinate the consortium's research with the members of #co-ops4dev,[127] the Overseas Cooperative Development Council, and other co-op development organizations.

Chapter 31

Cooperative Education

Personal experience

As a student, I had no access to courses on co-ops in secondary school nor as an undergraduate, and was only able to find one course on co-ops during my graduate studies. I had to make my own "major" in co-ops by piecing together somewhat-related courses, independent studies, and research for my dissertation on farming co-ops in Zambia.

As a teacher, I wove some information on co-ops into my sociology courses; was a trainer in several co-op development workshops; taught a co-op innovations course in a co-op master's program at Saint Mary's University in Halifax, Nova Scotia; and was part of a team that put together an international cooperative development manual for Land O'Lakes.[128]

The Inadequacy of cooperative education at almost all levels

Co-op education is a broad topic, encompassing what we learn about co-ops in primary and secondary schools, at the undergraduate and graduate school levels, and in other venues such as cooperative development training programs, conferences, in-person and on-line seminars, other online information sources, and in on-the-job training.

For example, in the United States there are more than 300 million cooperative and mutual memberships, and yet there is almost nothing taught about cooperatives at the secondary, college, and graduate school levels in social science, business, accounting, and law programs.

This problem exists in other countries as well, although not to the extreme extent as in the United States. But the basic point applies: far greater attention needs to be paid to teaching about democratic business forms in academic institutions and in cooperative development programs throughout the world.

There is a wide variation among countries and languages in terms of access to these different types of cooperative learning experiences. To my knowledge, there is no periodic, international evaluation of country-by-country access to co-op education.

RECOMMENDATION 5

Periodically conduct an international review of cooperative education, and develop strategies for greatly expanding access to it.

ICA or another apex co-op organization should coordinate a periodic review (for example, every five years) that would cover all the different types of cooperative education mentioned above. It would conclude by identifying particularly effective educational approaches, and presenting strategies and timetables for improving cooperative education around the world.

Chapter 32

Cooperative Laws and Regulations

This chapter presents two examples of not-very-successful cooperative law reform and implementation projects. It also describes two programs within the cooperative community that have good potential to carry out effective co-op legal and regulatory reform.

Cooperative law reform in Ghana

Papa Sene, CLUSA's West African Director, and I coordinated the Ghana Co-operative Law Reform Project in 2004. The project included four regional workshops and a national workshop to develop recommendations for changes in Ghana's co-op law, which dates back to the pre-independence days of British colonial rule before the late 1950s. We worked closely with the Ghana Co-operatives Council to work on the implementation of the proposed reforms. I prepared a case study report on the project so that the participatory approach used in Ghana could be adapted in other countries.

Altogether, well over 100 cooperators participated in the regional workshops and came up with dozens of proposed changes to Ghana's co-op law. The biggest complaints were how long it took to get a new co-op approved – often two years or more – and the arbitrary power of the registrar of cooperatives to interfere in the operations of a co-op. What was particularly validating about this process was that the results and recommendations were very similar across the four meetings.

We then collated the regional meeting results into a composite set of recommendations that was used to facilitate a meeting of the national co-op council. Again, the process went very well, with the national representatives being largely in agreement with the recommendations from the regional meetings. We then developed a proposed, revised national co-op law for consideration as a replacement to the old law.

Unfortunately, all of this hard work and consensus decision-making hit a major roadblock in Ghana's attorney general's office. For whatever reason, the proposed legislation was shelved there despite the lobbying efforts of Co-op Council members. Based on a recent review of the website of Ghana's Department of Cooperatives, the proposed co-op law is still gathering dust 15 years later, or even worse, may have ended up in the attorney general's waste basket.

Implementing a new set of co-op regulations in Bhutan

I presented a case study on Bhutan in Chapter 23. The punchline of the story was that bureaucratic inertia can be a huge impediment to cooperative development. When I was there in 2010, Bhutan was well-situated to launch an effective campaign to establish dozens of new forestry and farming co-ops under a newly adopted set of regulations. The Department of Cooperatives, however, chose to take an extremely go-slow approach to co-op development, largely based on the advice of overly cautious, expatriate advisors.

CLARITY

To quote from OCDC's website:

> The Cooperative Law and Regulation Initiative, CLARITY, was created in 2005 by the members of the U.S. Overseas Cooperative Development Council [OCDC], with support from the U.S. Agency for International Development. CLARITY grew from the shared experiences and convictions of OCDC's members that outmoded legal systems were barriers to cooperative development in many parts of the world. The goal of

CLARITY is to support cooperative movements as they analyze and change legal and regulatory environments. The result? To create an environment that enables cooperative businesses to flourish.

OCDC published four very useful reports between 2006 and 2013 as guides to carry out the law reform goals of CLARITY:

- Enabling Cooperative Development: Principles for Legal Reform[129]

- Creating CLARITY: Assessment, Analysis and Outreach for Cooperative Legal Reform[130]

- Applying the CLARITY Principles to the Nicaraguan Cooperative Law: Workshop Report[131]

- Cooperative Advocacy: A Practical Guide to Cooperative Legal and Regulatory Reform[132]

At the present time, OCDC does not appear to be actively implementing CLARITY. However, the guides that it developed continue to be a valuable set of tools for cooperative law reform.

ICA Cooperative Law Committee

Among a number of other issues related to cooperative law, the committee:

- "Assesses, advises on, proposes and monitors changes in cooperative policy at national, regional, international and global levels as they affect cooperative law.

- "Participate[s] in the establishment of implementation mechanisms, such as cooperative registration, monitoring and auditing."[133]

Hagen Henrÿ, the current chair of the committee, has written three editions of Guidelines for Cooperative Legislation, the most recent in 2012.[134] The book provides an excellent overview of the history of cooperative laws, and a step-by-step guide to forming country-level cooperative laws that conform to the ICA principles.

RECOMMENDATION 6

Conduct a comprehensive international review of cooperative laws and regulations, and develop a strategy and implementation timetable for country-level reform where needed.

This review should be overseen by the Cooperative Law Committee or a similar entity. It should be conducted by Euricse and/or other research bodies knowledgeable about the international cooperative community. The research tools and scoring system developed by OCDC's CLARITY project could play an important role in designing and implementing the research and reform project.

Note that this recommendation is consistent with several of the law-related actions proposed in ICA's *Blueprint for a Cooperative Decade.*[135]

Chapter 33

Cooperative Finance

Finance is a necessary ingredient for turning cooperative ideas into reality. In a nutshell, there are three kinds of finance: grants and donations, equity, and debt. This chapter does not go into detail on these different forms of finance, but rather makes some basic observations and recommendations about how the cooperative community can take steps to make better use of them, especially in developing countries.

Grants and donations

When the steering committee that formed Cooperative Development Services (CDS) in 1985 mapped out its strategy for making the organization operational, the members quickly realized that grants and donations would be needed to launch and sustain CDS. As described in Chapter 8, CDS was incorporated as a cooperative, but also has a tax-exempt division that allows it to receive tax-deductible grants and donations.

The fledgling organization was able to secure economic development grant funds from the State of Wisconsin and hired a professional fundraising firm to assist it in receiving donations from several large organizations in the U.S. cooperative community.

At first glance, one may not think that the start-up of a CDO in Wisconsin has any relevance to strengthening the international cooperative community. But I would argue that it definitely does. The scale is different, but the process of accessing grants and donations is very similar.

RECOMMENDATION 7

Establish an international cooperative education, research, and development foundation.

The International Cooperative Alliance should take the lead in forming the foundation. Three critical steps in launching such a foundation would be: the selection of a fundraising committee comprised of representatives from a diverse array of co-op sectors and countries; developing an appropriate legal structure for the foundation; and hiring a professional fundraising firm to conduct a survey of the CEOs of major co-ops, foundations, and other potential givers, and soliciting donations from them.

Survey responses would reveal the CEOs' priority goals for the foundation, and the amount of money they believe could be realistically raised for it. Three successful approaches that are well established in fundraising circles: use professional fundraisers to solicit donations; ask the leaders of the most prosperous organizations for generous contributions; and use the commitments of these leaders as peer pressure to secure other gifts. It is also important to structure the foundation sustainably, resulting in a pipeline of new financial support coming in on an ongoing basis.

Equity and debt

There have been a number of initiatives during the past decade to research the state of international financing for cooperatives, and to establish new international cooperative financial partnerships and instruments. However, a review of cooperative websites does not give a positive picture of the current state of these various initiatives.

The Global Cooperative Development Fund was established in 2012 (the UN's Year of the Cooperative). To quote one source from 2011:

> During the recent launch of the United Nations
> International Year of Co-operatives 2012 (IYC 2012),
> the worldwide co-operative movement also launched
> a new development fund – the Global Development
> Co-operative Fund (GDC) – to help provide much-
> needed finance to cooperatives in developing
> countries.[136]

However, it is not clear whether this fund ever became operational. In 2015, the Fund appears to have morphed into the Global Cooperative Impact (GCI) Fund and taken on an African cooperative development focus. According to ICA:

> The starting point for the strategy for a global co-oper-
> ative future is the powerful claim which co-operatives
> make to the outside world: that they have a way of doing
> business which is both better, and brings a more effec-
> tive balance to the global economy. The GCI Fund is

positioning itself as a lead institution to provide long term financing to co-operatives in developing countries so that they may be established, grow and flourish. Granting reliable and dedicated funding to co-operative models we build the cooperative identity and strongly encourage participation within membership and bring governance to a new level of consideration.[137]

Since this announcement in 2015, there have been very few references to this new fund on the web. One wonders whether it, too, has become defunct or, at best, dormant.

On the positive side, CoopMed is a financial initiative begun in 2016 that could serve as a model for other co-op development funds. Credit Cooperatif is its primary shareholder. According to CoopMed's website:

Social and economic innovation is key to reduce poverty, unemployment and inequalities that are eroding the social cohesion in the countries on the southern and eastern shores of the Mediterranean. Through its activities CoopMed aims to:

- Foster job creation and economic opportunities through the support of local financial actors

- Support initiatives for economic development promoted by the local civil society

- Fight climate change by promoting green and innovative initiatives

- Promote all forms of social economy initiatives: cooperatives, social, green and micro entrepreneurship[138]

RECOMMENDATION 8

Commission the development of a strategic plan for creating a network of cooperative financial institutions and other sources to finance cooperative business development in developing countries, and implement the plan.

ICA and other internationally oriented cooperative organizations have expressed interest in providing financial services to co-ops in developing countries during the past decade. However, with the exception of CoopMed, they have had limited success in doing so. Initiating a formal process for planning and implementing a set of financial services targeted to developing countries has potential to turn this goal into a successful initiative.

In developing such a co-op financing project, international cooperative leaders should also consider the potential for a financial initiative similar to GoFundMe [139] in which co-ops and co-op members around the world would become active in donating to, and investing in, co-op projects in developing countries.

Chapter 34

Cooperative Development Organizations

In Chapter 9, I presented a brief history of the ways in which cooperatives have been developed. Since the mid-1980s, an increasingly strong role has been played by domestic and international cooperative development organizations or CDOs, including Cooperative Development Services, with which I was involved for almost 30 years.

In the first two decades of the 21ˢᵗ century, I was a consultant to several international CDOs, primarily in Africa and Asia.

My experience with two African projects was as a colleague with staff members from four domestic cooperative development organizations that had been formed in Mali, Burkina Faso, and Benin with the assistance of CLUSA, and were operating independently as community-oriented research and development organizations. One project was an historical review of a community health initiative in Burkina Faso (discussed in Chapter 14). The other was an evaluation of mutual health organizations in Mali, Burkina Faso, and Benin (summarized in Chapter 15). Working with staff members of these organizations was invaluable, not only because of the translation skills that they brought to the projects, but also because of their knowledge of the local communities we visited.

In 2013, the Overseas Cooperative Development Council hired me to organize an international research division. OCDC is comprised of 10 member organizations all of which provide cooperative development assistance in developing countries. While at OCDC, I became familiar with Cooperatives in Development,[140] a European consortium of 10 internationally-oriented CDOs, and with four Canadian organizations providing international co-op assistance.[141]

Thus, I have had the opportunity to work with a variety of domestic and international cooperative development organizations. My overriding conclusion based on these various involvements with CDOs is that we need many more of them – in both developing and developed countries. These organizations are a key means to expanding the number of co-ops around the world, and to increasing the likelihood that these co-ops will be sustainable and a good fit with the local and national contexts in which they operate.

RECOMMENDATION 9

Form a network of international and domestic cooperative development organizations to prepare and implement a strategy to establish additional CDOs in countries throughout the world.

This network should be coordinated by the International Cooperative Alliance, Cooperatives in Development, the Overseas Cooperative Development Council, CooperationWorks!, the Canadian cooperative development community, CDOs based in developing countries and other organizations.

Chapter 35

Cooperation Among Cooperatives

As many of us are aware, "cooperation among cooperatives" is the sixth principal agreed upon by members of the International Cooperative Alliance in 1995. It states that:

> Co-operatives serve their members most effectively and strengthen the co-operative movement by working together through local, national, regional, and international structures.[142]

My favorite story about cooperation among cooperatives is mentioned in Chapter 25. As a reminder, the Norwegian cooperative, Felleskjøpet, provided financial support for a project in Mozambique that trained and assisted over 5,000 farmers to form co-ops and grow non-GMO soybeans. The project was a big success. The farmers proved to be very good soybean growers and were able to market all that they produced. However, their best market turned out be chicken farmers in Mozambique, and not the Norwegian co-op that had financed a big part of their success.

The reaction of the Norwegian co-op? Very positive. In fact, the co-op provided additional funding for soybean cultivation in Mozambique after the completion of the first project. In other words, the Norwegian co-op put the success of the Mozambican project above its own quest for soybeans. (Felleskjøpet ended up contracting with growers in Brazil to meet its soybean import needs.)

I wrote a report in 2013 entitled *Co-op to Co-op Trade: Linking Producer Cooperatives in Developing Countries with Consumer Cooperatives in Developed Countries*, and presented it at an ICA conference in South Africa. It reviewed the then-current state of this type of trade, particularly as it related to food products purchased from cooperatives of small-scale producers; drew lessons from the situation at the time; and made recommendations for increasing this type of trade in the future.

Slightly revised versions of these recommendations are presented below:

RECOMMENDATION 10

Launch a campaign to significantly increase the value of products sold by consumer co-ops in developed countries that are sourced from smallholder producer co-ops in developing countries.

The International Cooperative Alliance and cooperative development organizations should coordinate this campaign.

RECOMMENDATION 11

Establish a Cooperative Development Clearinghouse to coordinate and increase the availability of technical and financial assistance for the formation and ongoing support of smallholder agricultural co-ops in developing countries.

ICA, the Overseas Cooperative Development Council, Cooperatives in Development,[143] and other organizations involved in international cooperative development should play lead roles in coordinating and increasing assistance to smallholder farmers.

RECOMMENDATION 12

Develop strategies and measurable objectives to implement a wide range of co-op to co-op trade and other coordinated activities among cooperatives.[144]

ICA and other organizations involved in international cooperative development should plan and carry out this recommendation.

It is important to note that improving domestic and international trade by co-ops in general, and not just among co-ops, is a key part of strengthening the international cooperative community. For example, the long-term co-op development project in Indonesia and East Timor described in Chapter 27 provides an excellent example of international trade between co-ops and non-co-ops facilitated by CLUSA.

Chapter 36

Integrating the Cooperative Building Blocks

I referred to the components of this section of the book as "cooperative building blocks" for a reason. They are not standalone elements of any given cooperative or the cooperative movement more broadly. They need to stand together to make the co-op community strong.

Following are several examples illustrating the importance of combining these building blocks to create more effective approaches to cooperative development.

The Mondragon federation of cooperatives provides an excellent example of co-op entrepreneurship. It distinguishes itself by its integrated structure, combining financing through its own bank (a cooperative, member-owned financial institution), developing future co-op leaders through Mondragon University, and developing an entire infrastructure to support the cooperative community in the Mondragon area.

Self Help Africa, with the assistance of the Overseas Cooperative Development Council, carried out an applied research project to determine why malt barley co-op members in Ethiopia were selling some of their barley to outside buyers rather than to their co-ops. They used the information gathered in the research to reduce this "side selling." But that isn't the only distinguishing feature of Self Help Africa. This nonprofit has developed a strong fundraising capability in Europe and the United States to support its work in Africa, and has established an effective network of cooperative and community developers in a number of African countries.

Social co-ops began to make a significant impact in Italy in the 1970s, but it wasn't until 1991 and in subsequent years that the number of these co-ops proliferated as a result of a new Italian law defining them and giving them preferred status for providing social services. However, it is one thing to become legally recognized, and another to earn the trust and respect of the municipalities and clients with which these co-ops work. Their rapid growth in Italy and their spread to other European countries attest to their success in doing so.

The rise of credit unions and energy co-ops in the United States illustrate two very different ways in which co-op finance caused a co-op sector to take off. In the case of credit unions, this start-up movement was given a big sendoff by the donation of $1 million from Edward Filene in 1920. But it wasn't just this donation that caused credit unions to grow rapidly during the next 30 years and beyond. The leaders of the Credit Union National Extension Bureau used these funds to support the passage of state-level credit union laws, and to organize thousands of credit unions across the country.

As mentioned at the beginning of this section, the big financial impediment to getting electricity to rural areas in the United States was the cost of transmitting it over long, sparsely populated distances. That problem was solved by a low-interest lending program created by the Rural Electrification Act in 1936. However, the availability of this loan program was only part of the picture. Hundreds of rural communities needed to mobilize themselves to create co-ops and sign up members.

The building blocks identified in this chapter are essential to forming and maintaining successful cooperatives. And yet, because co-ops are run by and for their members, and face different obstacles to success, each co-op and each co-op sector have unique characteristics and paths to sustainability that place very different emphases on the application of the building blocks.

International Cooperative Growth Opportunities, 2021-2030

The current decade, 2021-2030, provides numerous opportunities to apply the building blocks discussed in the previous section and to grow the cooperative movement in ways that benefit people around the world. This section of the book focuses on how the number of co-ops and co-op memberships can increase exponentially in this decade and beyond. An estimated 1 billion people are already members of co-ops. With effective leadership and commitment of resources by the international cooperative community, that number could double by 2030.

Chapter 37 emphasizes the role that strategic planning can play in expanding the number of co-ops and co-op memberships. Chapter 38 identifies several opportunities for co-op growth in combating climate change. Chapter 39 describes co-op growth opportunities in community health. Chapter 40 provides a synopsis of this section of the book.

Many of the opportunities identified address the UN Sustainable Development Goals (mentioned in Chapter 29) intended to be accomplished between 2016 and 2030.[145]

Chapter 37

Realizing Co-op Opportunities Through Strategic Analysis and Coordinated Development

As I have stressed throughout the book, co-ops don't just happen. People need to organize and participate in them. A common pattern in the history of the cooperative movement has been that co-ops are formed when for-profit businesses and/or the public sector have failed to address important human needs.

In the future, those of us in the co-op community should be more proactive in the way that we approach the development of new cooperatives. It is good to fill gaps left by for-profits and government agencies, but it is also important to plan ahead and address human needs proactively.

This chapter lays out an approach to co-op development based on proactive, strategic planning. If we in the co-op community increase this type of cooperative entrepreneurial development, we can augment the number of co-op memberships by the hundreds of millions in the next decade and more effectively address problems of economic and social justice.

1. **Develop targeted strategies for co-op sectors, countries, and job-creation opportunities.** Rapidly expanding the number of co-op memberships by 2030 can happen only if factors such as better measurement; improved legal environments; community, governmental, foundation, and international support; and cooperative development assistance all increase dramatically.

   In addition, we need to think strategically about where to focus development resources. For example, insurance co-ops and mutuals, and financial cooperatives are using systematic development strategies that result in significant growth. Similar approaches should be applied in other co-op sectors.

The rapid expansion of cooperative businesses has to be planned, funded, implemented, evaluated, and periodically revised. For this to happen, the International Co-operative Alliance and others in the co-op community will need to play lead development roles.

2. **What is the potential for co-op growth in different countries?** The 2014 global co-op census estimates that India has about 265 million co-op memberships, equivalent to approximately 20 percent of its population. There are 136 million co-op memberships in China, equivalent to about 10 percent of its population. The same data set shows only about 2 million co-op memberships in Indonesia, equivalent to between 1 and 2% percent of its population.[146]

    What explains these differences? Are there co-op sectors in China and Indonesia (e.g., finance, insurance, farming, and/or others) that are ripe for rapid expansion? If so, how best can these opportunities be realized? China is the largest country in the world and has one of the fastest-growing economies. Indonesia is the fourth-largest country and its economy also is growing at a fairly rapid pace. Significant growth of the cooperative movement in these two countries would translate into hundreds of millions of new co-op memberships. Systematic analysis of the potential for cooperative growth should be done for other countries and regions of the world as well, not just those with the largest populations.

    As mentioned above, it appears that both financial co-ops and insurance co-ops and mutuals have been growing rapidly and have good potential to continue to do so, especially as the number of people living in extreme poverty diminishes.

3. **What is the potential for new and expanded agricultural co-ops in developing countries?** I recommended in Chapter 35 on co-op to co-op trade that a priority goal in the next decade should be to assist subsistence and subsistence-plus farmers to convert to small-scale commercial agriculture. Almost 90 percent of the world's 570 million farms are located in low-and middle-income countries. Agricultural supply, marketing, and service co-ops have a long history of success in developed countries and in some developing countries, such as India and Kenya.

Many examples, including several described in this book, have shown the ability of co-ops to help poor farmers transition to small-scale commercial farming. Tens of millions of farmers could become new members of co-ops in the next 10 years.

4. **How can the roles of employee-owned cooperatives, social co-ops, and multi-stakeholder co-ops (owned by multiple categories of members) expand during the next decade?** In a few countries, such as Spain, Italy, and France, these types of cooperatives are a significant part of the co-op economy, but on a world scale, they account for a very small percentage of co-ops and co-op memberships. Mondragon in Spain has shown the way to success by creating an integrated support system for its member co-ops and other organizations. Such a support system does not have to be limited to an internally coordinated set of building blocks as with Mondragon. A combination of external and internal incentives and sources of technical and financial assistance have propelled the rapid expansion of social enterprises in the European Union. Where there is a joint commitment by the cooperative community and the public sector, as in addressing sustainable development goals, there are opportunities for coordinated strategies for rapid growth.

RECOMMENDATION 13
Conduct and implement comprehensive strategies to realize cooperative growth opportunities around the world.

Strategic analyses should be conducted on an ongoing basis under the auspices of ICA, ICETT, the cooperative section of the International Labour Organization,[147] and/or other international cooperative organizations. They should be accompanied by plans of action and measurable five- and 10-year objectives.

Chapter 38

Co-ops and Climate Change

Co-ops and climate change

The United States and many other countries have been slow to develop effective policies to take action against what is potentially the greatest environmental disaster that the world has faced since humans emerged as a species. Scientists are almost unanimous in concluding that greenhouse gas emissions are reaching a tipping point that is already causing increasing world temperatures and deadly weather-related events, including droughts, desertification, floods, rising sea levels, tornadoes, forest and grass fires, and other effects.[148]

Because of their unique values, principles, and organizational structure, cooperatives can play a lead role in mitigating the harmful impacts of global warming in the United States and in other countries. In theory, if not always in practice, cooperatives are service organizations, committed to sustainable development, and have the ability to mobilize large numbers of people to act on their own behalf and that of their neighbors. The rapid growth of the mutual insurance industry, credit unions, and agricultural and rural electric cooperatives illustrates the power and speed of cooperation as an organizing activity.

This mobilizing ability can be applied to reducing the harmful effects of global warming. Two examples of applying the power of cooperation to problems related to climate change are presented in this chapter: community solar cooperatives and forestry cooperatives.

Community solar cooperatives

I presented a paper in the spring of 2019 at the Association of Cooperative Educators Institute entitled "Community Solar Cooperatives in Developing Countries."[149] Following are some excerpts and findings from the paper.

The purpose of the paper was to contribute to the goal of achieving worldwide electrification by 2030 by increasing the development of community solar cooperatives that provide electricity through mini-grids and solar installations on individual homes and other buildings.

There are almost a billion people who have no access to electricity, living primarily in Africa, Asia, and Latin America. That's one-seventh of the world's population. There are hundreds of millions more whose energy is unreliable, dirty, unhealthy, inadequate, unsustainable, and/or expensive – for example, kerosene, diesel, wood, and candles.[150]

Almost every country in the world has made a commitment through the United Nations Paris Agreement to significantly cut back by 2030 on their use of energy sources that emit carbon dioxide into the atmosphere.

These same countries have made commitments through the UN's Sustainable Development Goals program to dramatically improve the quality of life around the world by 2030, in part by ensuring "access to affordable, reliable, sustainable, and modern energy for all."[151]

There are many ways in which universal access to electricity will improve the quality of people's lives – for example, creating job opportunities, reducing the workload of women by saving, on average, an hour a day that is currently spent searching for firewood, and preventing almost 2 million premature deaths per year from household air pollution. There would also be a net reduction in greenhouse gas emissions because of lower use of biomass fuel for cooking, and the virtual elimination of kerosene and other dirty fuels as sources of heat and light.[152]

How can the ambitious goal of "electricity for all" be realized?

The broad answer is to dramatically increase the use of decentralized, renewable energy to meet the world's unmet and under-met needs for electricity. Since most people without electricity do not have access to transmission lines, the most feasible approach to providing them with electricity is through community solar mini-grids[153] and single-building installations, many of which could be organized as cooperatives.

Many of the close-to-a-billion people who don't have access to electricity live in fairly remote areas that are not easily connected to major power grids. As a result, large-scale renewable options don't apply to them and are not likely to in the near future because of the high cost of transmission lines.

In these off-the-grid locations, households and businesses, and clusters of energy consumers at the village level, can be most economically and efficiently served by electricity generated locally. Following are two examples of decentralized approaches.

The Totota Co-op in rural Liberia began operating a solar mini-grid in 2018. With a contract from the U.S. Agency for International Development, the National Rural Electric Cooperative Association (NRECA) and Bandera Electric Co-op (one of NRECA's member cooperatives) assisted the Liberian village with organizing the co-op and installing solar panels, a battery-storage unit, and other equipment. NRECA is also working with 12 Liberian coastal villages to expand the community solar model to them.[154]

Kenya has a much higher distribution of electricity than most Sub-Saharan African countries. Approximately 75% of Kenyans have access to electricity from grid and off-grid sources, according to the World Bank. The Kenyan government wants to increase that to 100% by 2022. The Kenya National Electrification Strategy (KNES) references mini-grids, independent solar power plants, and off-grid technology as options to utilize. About 49 million people live in Kenya, and most of them are in rural areas.[155]

One of the options being pursued in Kenya is a private-sector partnership between Azuri, Unilever, and local community residents. In this program, households and businesses purchase solar kits via a rent-to-buy system. Purchasers make monthly payments for 18 months, and then they own the kits outright. The kits come in various sizes, from a single light set-up to one that can power multiple lights and other appliances, including a television. Another feature of the distribution system is that local community residents are trained to sell, install, and maintain the kits. Thus, there is a direct, local employment impact as well as the indirect economic, social, health, and educational benefits resulting from increased access to energy.[156] This Azuri/Unilever model has excellent potential to be adapted for use by community solar co-ops in other developing countries.

The paper draws two key conclusions:

1. Community solar cooperatives are already in place in some developing countries and could be expanded rapidly to provide electricity in many more.

2. Unless the expansion of these co-ops becomes a much higher priority of the international cooperative community and of international development organizations, the huge potential for these local, democratically run, renewable energy providers will not be realized.

RECOMMENDATION 14

Rapidly expand the development of solar cooperatives in the rural communities of developing countries.

This should take place under the auspices of the International Cooperative Alliance with the National Rural Electric Cooperative Association and other international and domestic cooperative development organizations taking lead roles in designing and implementing the initiative.

Community forestry co-ops

A May 2019 article in UN News stated that:

> [P]rotection and enhancing the world's forests is one of the most cost-effective forms of climate action: forests act as carbon sinks, absorbing roughly 2 billion metric tonnes [2.2 billion U.S. tons] of carbon dioxide each year. Sustainable forest management can build resilience and help mitigate and adapt to climate change.[157]

In 2011 (revised in 2016), my son Luc Nadeau and I prepared a paper entitled, "The role of forestry cooperatives in climate change mitigation" for presentation at an International Cooperative Alliance-sponsored conference in Finland. The purpose of the paper was to analyze how forestry cooperatives can play an important role in reducing the emission of carbon dioxide into the atmosphere in both developing and developed countries. The paper made the case that by 2030:

> Forestry cooperatives could become the primary means by which the world's carbon emissions from deforestation are reduced and the storage of carbon in forests is increased. The underlying contention of the paper is that forestry co-ops have a unique ability to efficiently aggregate and mobilize large numbers of people and resources at the community level in order to increase net forest carbon sequestration.[158]

Following are several bullet points that summarize key contents of the paper:

- Forests constitute more than 4 billion hectares, or about 31% of the earth's total land area,[159] and store about two-thirds of terrestrial carbon. About 3 billion hectares have been lost to deforestation and degradation.[160]

- A United Nations program asserts that stabilizing global temperatures "will be practically impossible to achieve without reducing emissions from the forest sector, in addition to other mitigation actions."[161] Deforestation and forest-degradation release are responsible for about 12% of total anthropogenic carbon dioxide emissions.[162]

- There is broad agreement among scientists and political leaders that, if effective international policies and incentives are put in place [by 2030], the world's forests could become a major source of increased carbon storage and one of the most cost-effective ways to slow the amount of carbon dioxide going into the atmosphere.[163]

- A key concept that is often discussed in relation to forest carbon sequestration is "payment for ecosystem services" or PES. PES programs provide a "source of income for land management, restoration, conservation, and sustainable use activities."[164] Similar to other goods and services, storage of carbon in forests is a product that can be bought and sold. Landowners and land managers can be paid to maintain or increase the amount of carbon stored in forestland. On a worldwide scale, these payments can be the cornerstone of an international initiative to sequester billions of additional tons of carbon in forests.

- Two types of community forestry co-ops have the potential to provide the ecosystem services described above:

  - Forest-owner cooperatives are owned and democratically controlled by individuals, families, and organizations that own forestland. They provide a variety of services to their landowner-members, especially forest management services and timber marketing services. They have a long history in Western Europe and can also be found in Canada, the United States, Japan, and other developed countries.[165] Some agricultural cooperatives also provide forestry services to their members.[166]

♦ Forest-user cooperatives, also referred to as community forest management groups, are comprised of local residents who make use of state-owned or communal forests for firewood, charcoal, timber, non-timber forest products, hunting, eco-tourism, and other activities. For the most part, these groups are committed to sustainable forest management. They are most likely to be found in Central and South America, Africa, and Asia.[167] It is important to note that most of these groups are not registered as cooperatives, although they generally meet the basic cooperative criterion of being democratically controlled by their members.

• The paper presents examples from the United States, the European Union, Mexico, Senegal, and the Himalayan countries of Nepal and Bhutan that illustrate how carbon sequestration projects could be carried out by forestry cooperatives and similar organizations in very different ecological, economic, political, and land-tenure contexts.

RECOMMENDATION 15

Greatly expand the role of community forestry cooperatives in carrying out carbon sequestration projects in both developing and developed countries.

The ICA, the United Nations Programme on Reducing Emissions from Deforestation and Forest Degradation,[168] *and international and domestic cooperative development organizations should oversee the expanded environmental role of these co-ops, especially the design and implementation of systems for payment of ecosystem services resulting in increased carbon sequestration.*

Chapter 39

Community Health Cooperatives

I referred to my paper, "The First Mile: The Potential for Community-Based Health Cooperatives in Sub-Saharan Africa"[169] in Chapter 16. Following are some excerpts and findings from the paper, emphasizing the important benefits of these co-ops and their potential for rapid expansion in the current decade.

> The paper presents a model for community-based health cooperatives that is based to a large extent on a successful community health mobilization program in Kenya.[170] The paper briefly reviews the persistence of serious health problems on the subcontinent and then presents the cooperative model as an effective means to address health and health-delivery issues in the region. The paper concludes by calling for broader application of the cooperative health model and for rigorous research to document changes in health and mortality indicators in communities served by these cooperatives. The paper also includes two appendices that contain focus group and case study results on the community health-mobilization program carried out in the western and coast provinces of Kenya.

> By mobilizing community residents to take the lead role in their own health planning and service provision, community-based health cooperatives in Sub-Saharan Africa have the potential to play a critical role in improving health conditions on the subcontinent.

> Among international donors and health providers, a widely acknowledged frustration is the difficulty of getting assistance to rural communities that are often

the most in need of health services.[171] This gap is sometimes referred to as the "last mile" problem. From the
village perspective, this same mile is the "first mile"
toward accessing health services. This paper proposes
that community health cooperatives provide a means
for villagers themselves to define their priority health
needs and to play the lead role in addressing them. These
co-ops have the potential to bridge the "last mile" gap
by creating a "first mile" capability at the village level to
take care of basic health problems and to reach out to the
health delivery system when greater assistance is needed.

The community-based health cooperative model

How can health services be delivered to villagers
dispersed across the countryside?[172] This is where the
community health cooperative model comes into play.
The model takes a comprehensive, village-by-village
approach to health problems and solutions. It focuses
on the portion of the population that the current system
is least equipped to serve. And it mobilizes community
residents to take the lead role in their own health planning and service provision.

The model does not assume that village organizations can
solve all of their health problems by themselves. Village
health co-ops would need to work with public and
private health providers. They would need health education, services, and pharmaceutical supplies from outside
the local community. However, the biggest gap in current
health delivery systems – between health providers and
residents of rural communities – would be bridged by
villagers meeting their own basic health education and
service needs and, when appropriate, by seeking health
services from outside the community in an organized
manner, instead of relying on an understaffed and

underfunded health system to reach out to them.

The CLUSA example in Kenya

In 2001, CLUSA, the international program of the National Cooperative Business Association, began providing community health mobilization services in rural Kenya. Since its first project began in western Kenya, CLUSA has assisted more than 2,000 communities to form village, multi-village, women's, and youth-based health associations and to develop and implement community health plans. CLUSA has also trained more than 4,000 village-based, community health workers. Altogether, more than 1 million community residents in Kenya have benefited from this program.[173]

This paper [makes] a case for the application of a community-based health cooperative model in Sub-Saharan Africa. Key potential benefits of the broad application of such a model on the subcontinent are:

- Addressing the "last mile" problem – the persistent inability of current healthcare delivery systems to effectively reach village residents

- The potential of village-based cooperatives to be first responders to, and "first mile" providers of, health education and healthcare

- The experience of CLUSA's community health programs in Kenya from 2001 through 2012

- The ability to modify the CLUSA approach into the development of community-based healthcare cooperatives

- The low cost and the potential for rapid expansion and sustainability of the model

Tens of millions of lives are at stake in rapidly identifying and implementing effective ways to improve health
conditions in rural communities of the region. Village-
based co-ops have the potential to be a key part of a
health-delivery strategy that could be put in place quickly
and on a broad scale.

It is interesting to note that the results of focus groups I conducted
indicated a broad definition of "health" by many of the partici-
pants. For example, a number of them listed sanitation, "dirty
water," bad roads, and poverty as health issues. One takeaway from
these responses is that community-development cooperatives as
well as community health co-ops may be desirable in some of the
villages in order to address these broader needs.

RECOMMENDATION 16
Develop an initiative to establish community health cooperatives in rural areas of Africa, Latin America, and Asia that currently lack adequate
healthcare services.

*This initiative should be coordinated through the International Cooper-
ative Alliance, the United Nations Department of Economic and Social
Affairs, CLUSA, the Gates Foundation,[174] and organizations involved in
promoting healthcare in developing countries.*

Chapter 40

Review of Cooperative Growth Opportunities

This section of the book has identified several examples of cooperative initiatives that should be launched between 2021 and 2030. The list of initiatives is not intended to be comprehensive, but rather to represent important co-op opportunities that have large growth potential in the current decade.

Some examples represent proactive approaches by the broader cooperative community to address strategically identified growth opportunities in well-established cooperative sectors such as insurance, finance, agriculture, employee ownership, and social services.

The examples also include co-ops providing services that require greatly expanded attention, such as community solar co-ops, forestry co-ops focused on carbon sequestration, and community health co-ops. All of these latter opportunities are intended to be part of the implementation of the UN Sustainable Development Goal Program.

Taken together, these two types of initiatives could benefit well over a billion people around the world, potentially more than doubling the current number of cooperative memberships.

Conclusion: Strengthening the International Cooperative Community in the 21st Century

This book is a combination of lessons learned from my personal experiences in the world of co-ops during the past 50 years; historical and contemporary observations of the broader co-op community; and recommendations derived from these experiences and observations.

The book begins with a recounting of my introduction to co-ops in 1970. This personal story is followed by several historical reviews of development in different cooperative sectors and changes in the process of cooperative development over time. Then I present a set of brief case studies of international co-op development projects, all but one of which I participated in directly. The next section discusses the building blocks of cooperative development. The book's final section presents examples of cooperative opportunities that could be realized between 2021 and 2030, potentially doubling co-op memberships around the world to 2 billion. These last two sections also contain 16 recommendations for action by the international cooperative community and other organizations during the current decade.

Concluding thoughts

One could argue that the primary historical role of cooperatives has been to fill the gaps left unfilled by for-profit enterprises and neglectful governments. There is nothing wrong with this role. After all, people need protection from fires, safe places to save and borrow money, fair prices for their agricultural inputs and outputs, sustainable jobs, and access to affordable goods and services.

However, this fill-the-gap approach is just one of the functions of cooperatives. In fact, I would argue that in the 21st century, co-ops should shift from primarily playing a gap-filler role to instead becoming innovative, proactive leaders in building a more equitable and just world economy and society.

For example, climate change currently threatens the well-being of every person in the world, and the environmental sustainability of the planet itself. The cooperative community acknowledges the importance of this crisis, but, realistically, what has it done about it? I would argue: not much.

Similarly, International co-op leaders voice support for the United Nations Sustainable Development Goals (which include "Climate Action"). But, what have they done to address them? Again, I would argue: not much.

Three big limitations hindering the co-op community from playing a stronger role in the world economy are that:

- Co-op leaders have tended to see cooperative development as primarily filling gaps rather than as cooperative entrepreneurship.

- There are no entities within the co-op world designed to take the lead in carrying out broad new entrepreneurial initiatives. (The International Cooperative Entrepreneurship Think Tank [ICETT] may be a significant step in correcting this. However, I hope it evolves into a "do tank" as well as a "think tank.")

- There are no strong cross-cooperative mechanisms to bring together finances, technology, and other co-op building blocks to implement such initiatives.

As history has shown, some of the best co-op initiatives have involved a number of diverse components: clear demand by consumers, producers, and jobseekers or employees; systematic organizing strategies; solid research; effective legislation and regulation; educational campaigns; and structures for sustaining co-ops once created.

Two major challenges face the international cooperative community: to increase its proactive, development skills, and to reshape the cooperative movement to meet the needs of the 21st century. This restructured movement would successfully challenge the profit-dominated world economy and demonstrate the power of businesses that put service ahead of greed.

The numerous development lessons and 16 recommendations for strengthening the cooperative community, located throughout the book, are intended to identify practical steps that we can carry out in the current decade – and beyond.

Select the ones that are of most interest to you, and let's get going on implementing them.

Appendix A

Cooperative Identity, Values & Principles

This appendix provides an excerpt from the website of the International Cooperative Alliance that defines what a cooperative is, lists cooperative values, and defines the seven cooperative principles.[175]

Definition of a Cooperative

A cooperative is an autonomous association of persons united voluntarily to meet their common economic, social, and cultural needs and aspirations through a jointly-owned and democratically-controlled enterprise.

· · · · ·

Cooperative values

Cooperatives are based on the values of self-help, self-responsibility, democracy, equality, equity, and solidarity. In the tradition of their founders, cooperative members believe in the ethical values of honesty, openness, social responsibility and caring for others.

Cooperative Principles

The cooperative principles are guidelines by which cooperatives put their values into practice.

1. Voluntary and open membership

Cooperatives are voluntary organisations, open to all persons able to use their services and willing to accept the responsibilities of membership, without gender, social, racial, political or religious discrimination.

2. Democratic member control

Cooperatives are democratic organisations controlled by their members, who actively participate in setting their policies and making decisions. Men and women serving as elected representatives are accountable to the membership. In primary cooperatives members have equal voting rights (one member, one vote) and cooperatives at other levels are also organised in a democratic manner.

3. Member economic participation

Members contribute equitably to, and democratically control, the capital of their cooperative. At least part of that capital is usually the common property of the cooperative. Members usually receive limited compensation, if any, on capital subscribed as a condition of membership. Members allocate surpluses for any or all of the following purposes: developing their cooperative, possibly by setting up reserves, part of which at least would be indivisible;

benefiting members in proportion to their transactions with the cooperative; and supporting other activities approved by the membership.

4. Autonomy and Independence

Cooperatives are autonomous, self-help organisations controlled by their members. If they enter into agreements with other organisations, including governments, or raise capital from external sources, they do so on terms that ensure democratic control by their members and maintain their cooperative autonomy.

5. Education, training, and Information

Cooperatives provide education and training for their members, elected representatives, managers, and employees so they can contribute effectively to the development of their co-operatives. They inform the general public – particularly young people and opinion leaders – about the nature and benefits of co-operation.

6. Cooperation among cooperatives

Cooperatives serve their members most effectively and strengthen the cooperative movement by working together through local, national, regional and international structures.

7. Concern for community

Cooperatives work for the sustainable development of their communities through policies approved by their members.

Appendix B

Types of Cooperatives

Co-ops come in a wide range of sizes and serve diverse memberships.

Consumer cooperatives are the most common type of co-op in the world. Credit unions and mutual insurance companies are defined as consumer co-ops in this book because of their democratic ownership and voting structures. Members of consumer co-ops purchase goods and services from them, for example financial services through credit unions, insurance through mutual insurance companies, groceries through food co-ops, and so on.

Many of us have heard of co-ops owned by farmers. These *producer cooperatives* exist in almost every country in the world. Farmers purchase agricultural supplies from their co-ops, and sell grain, livestock, and produce through them. People who own forested land sometimes form co-ops in order to buy seedlings and other inputs, receive management assistance, and market forest products. Artists and craftspeople also own producer co-ops to purchase supplies and facilitate the sale of their art and craft products.

Co-ops owned by their employees, also called *worker co-ops*, represent another ownership model. The most famous example is the Mondragon Cooperative Corporation headquartered in the Basque region of Spain. This co-op federation is comprised of well over 200 co-ops and other businesses. Altogether these companies employ more than 80,000 people, most of whom are co-op owners. The primary service that a worker cooperative provides to its members is employment, which includes a democratic voice in the decision-making of the company.

Small businesses and other organizations also form cooperatives in order to purchase supplies and services that meet the members' specifications and can sometimes be bought at discounted prices. Businesses can also sell products or services through co-ops or engage in joint advertising in order to get higher returns or to reach markets that the individual businesses would not be able to access. For example, some hotels, restaurants, and hardware stores join together through co-ops or quasi-co-ops.

There is a fifth type of cooperative, sometimes called a *hybrid co-op or a multi-stakeholder co-op*. In these organizations, members come from a variety of categories – consumers, producers, workers, and/or small businesses. For example, there are a large number of social co-ops in Italy in which both employees and consumers are members. [176]

Appendix C

An Overview of my Career in Co-ops

In the Introduction, you read about my first experience with cooperatives as a Peace Corps volunteer in Senegal. After returning from the Peace Corps, I started graduate school in sociology at the University of Wisconsin in 1972. I "majored" in cooperatives in a program that did not have one course on co-ops. I did this by taking courses in other departments, especially agricultural economics, by convincing faculty members to let me do "independent study" courses on cooperatives, and by doing my dissertation on farming cooperatives in Zambia.

Getting a co-op job I didn't apply for

I spent a few years after receiving my Ph.D. in 1977 teaching sociology courses and working on a variety of projects and short-term jobs involving cooperatives, community development, and job creation. Then I had a major breakthrough at the end of 1984.

I was invited to interview for a job I wasn't aware existed and for which I hadn't applied.

Rod Nilsestuen, then the Executive Director of the Wisconsin Federation of Cooperatives, had seen the resume I had submitted for another job. He noticed my co-op background and thought I might be a good fit for a position he was creating at the Federation.

The job? Coordinating the formation of a cooperative development organization in Wisconsin. Nilsestuen interviewed me in December 1984. I became the Federation's director of cooperative development in January 1985. Six months later we incorporated the Wisconsin Cooperative Development Council. By the end of the year, the Council had raised enough public and private seed funding to begin operation – with me as its first executive director.

I served as the executive director for six years until the Council merged with North Country Cooperative Development Services and was renamed Cooperative Development Services, Inc. (CDS) with an expanded mission to serve Minnesota and Iowa (and other states as opportunities arose) as well as Wisconsin. I continued as the director of research, planning, and development for CDS until 2000.

Along the way, I co-authored a book with David J. Thompson entitled *Cooperation Works!* in 1997.[177]

In 2000, I changed my role with CDS from employee to consultant, a relationship that continued through 2013.

Back to Africa after a 27-year gap

Aside from a year in France on a Fulbright scholarship in the mid-1980s, a co-op evaluation project in Poland in 1991, and a whirlwind, four-country research project on sustainable food marketing in Europe in 1998, I had not been involved in the international cooperative development world since the 1970s. This changed dramatically in 2000 when I was hired as a consultant to provide organizational development assistance to two groups of agricultural co-ops in Zambia. This was the first of more than 25 international co-op consulting projects, primarily in Africa and Asia, during the next 18 years.

Other cooperative work since 2000

My work with co-ops has continued during the past 20 years as a teacher, researcher, writer, and developer. Some of these activities show up in the case studies and recommendations that I make in the book.

Following are a few highlights:

- Publication in 2012 of *The Cooperative Solution: How the United States can tame recessions, reduce inequality, and protect the environment*

- Director of research for the Overseas Cooperative Development Council in 2014 and 2015

- Formation of The Cooperative Society Project[178] in 2015. This is an ongoing, non-profit initiative with two goals:

  - To analyze the hypothesis that humans may be on the threshold of a new historical stage – one characterized by cooperation, democracy, the equitable distribution of resources, and a sustainable relationship with nature

  - To make recommendations for how we can increase the likelihood of moving toward a more cooperative society during the next several decades

- The primary activities of The Cooperative Society Project have been the publication in 2016 of *The Cooperative Society: The Next Stage of Human History*, and of its second edition in 2018, both co-authored with Luc Nadeau, along with a bimonthly eNewsletter. You are invited to visit our website at: thecooperativesociety.org

E.G. Nadeau, Ph.D.

Endnotes

Endnotes with hyperlinks were all active on February 1, 2021.

1. A brief overview of my co-op career is presented in Appendix C.

2. Côté, Daniel, *Cooperative Management: An Effective Model Adapted to Future Challenges*, Editions JFD, Jan 1, 2019.

3. "Facts and Figures," ICA, retrieved August 2020, https://www.ica.coop/en/cooperatives/facts-and-figures

4. For example: https://www.ica.coop/en; https://www.ilo.org/global/topics/cooperatives/lang--en/index.htm; https://community-wealth.org/strategies/panel/coops/index.html

5. Knapp, Joseph, *The Rise of American Cooperative Enterprise: 1620-1920*, Interstate Printers and Publishers, 1969, pp. 5-6.

6. "Ile d'Orleans," retrieved August 2020, http://tourisme.iledorleans.com/en/ile-d-orleans/founding-families-of-ile-d-orleans/

7. Note that these case studies are not comprehensive. For example, the important sector of housing co-ops is not reviewed in this section.

8. Isaacson, Walter, *Benjamin Franklin: An American Life*, New York: Simon & Schuster, 2003.

9. Knapp, 1969, op. cit. pp. 7-9.

10. Knapp, 1969, op. cit., p. 445.

11. "Mutual Insurance," National Association of Mutual Insurance Companies, retrieved October 2020, https://www.namic.org/about/mutualins

12. Knapp, 1969, op. cit., p., 94.

13. Knapp, 1969, op. cit., p. 13.

14. Knapp, 1969, op. cit., pp. 422-423

15. Deller, Steven, et al., Research on the Economic Impact of Cooperatives, University of Wisconsin Center for Cooperatives, Revised June 19, 2009, p. 38, https://resources.uwcc.wisc.edu/Research/REIC_FINAL.pdf

16. Global Mutual Market Share 10, ICMIF, 2018, https://www.icmif.org/publications/global-mutual-market-share/global-mutual-market-share-10

17. "How Rochdale Pioneers changed commerce forever," BBC, July 10, 2010, http://news.bbc.co.uk/local/manchester/hi/people_and_places/history/newsid_8838000/8838778.stmRochdale

18. "History," Willy Street Co-op, retrieved August 2020, https://www.willystreet.coop/about-us/willy-street-co-op-history

19. "About us," National Co+op Grocers, retrieved August 2020, https://www.ncg.coop/about-us

20. Deller, op. cit., p. 19-21.

21. Bosteels, Karin, "Swiss supermarket giants Coop and Migros are doing great", Food, March 28, 2019, https://www.retaildetail.eu/en/news/food/swiss-supermarket-giants-coop-and-migros-are-doing-great

22. "Food and grocery co-ops," NCBA CLUSA, retrieved August 2020, https://ncbaclusa.coop/resources/co-op-sectors/food-and-grocery-co-ops/

23. Dave Grace and Associates, Measuring the Size and Scope of the Cooperative Economy: Results of the 2014 Global Census on Co-operatives, April 2014, p. 5, https://www.un.org/esa/socdev/documents/2014/coopsegm/grace.pdf

24. "Friedrich Wilhelm Raiffeisen," Wikipedia, retrieved August 2020, https://en.wikipedia.org/wiki/Friedrich_Wilhelm_Raiffeisen; "Franz Hermann Schulze-Delitzsch," retrieved August 2020, https://en.wikipedia.org/wiki/Franz_Hermann_Schulze-Delitzsch

25. World Cooperative Monitor 2019, Euricse/International Cooperative Alliance, January 23, 2020, https://monitor.coop/en/media/library/research-and-reviews/world-cooperative-monitor-2019

26. "Quarterly Credit Union Data Summary," National Credit Union Administration, 2020, Q1, https://www.ncua.gov/files/publications/analysis/quarterly-data-summary-2020-Q1.pdf

27. Knapp, 1969, op. cit., pp. 140-141.

28. Knapp, Joseph G, *The Advance of American Cooperative Enterprise: 1920-1940*, 1973, p. 196.

29. Ibid., p. 196.

30. Ibid., p. 451.

31. "Quarterly Credit Union Data Summary," 2020, Q1, op. cit.

32. WOCCU Statistical Report, 2018, https://www.woccu.org/documents/2018_Statistical_Report

33. Dave Grace and Associates, op. cit., p. 5.

34. "Agricultural Cooperatives, Origins," Wikipedia, retrieved August 2020, https://en.wikipedia.org/wiki/Agricultural_cooperative#Origins

35. Nadeau, op. cit., p. 49.

36. Knapp, 1969, op. cit., pp. 46-47.

37. Knapp, 1969, op. cit., pp. 83-87.

38. "About," Sunkist, 2012. http://www.sunkist.com/about

39. Knapp, 1973, op. cit., pp. 3-4.

40. Deller, op. cit., p.16.

41. It is important not to forget that these farmers were preceded by Native Americans, many of whom had been practicing agriculture for thousands of years before they were often violently displaced by recently arrived Europeans. "Agriculture, American Indian," Encyclopedia.com, retrieved August 2020, https://www.encyclopedia.com/history/dictionaries-thesauruses-pictures-and-press-releases/agriculture-american-indian

42. Nor should we forget that, primarily in the southern United States, slaves of African origin provided the workforce for large-scale agricultural production in tobacco, cotton, and other cash crops. In fact, there were two systems of agriculture in the United States: one carried out by small-scale farmers and one dominated by large-scale, slave-based plantations. Even after the end of the Civil War, the South continued to have a pattern of agriculture that echoed the slave system that existed prior to the war. The predominant post-civil war approach to perpetuating racial inequality in agriculture was sharecropping, in which a large proportion of agricultural products produced by sharecroppers were appropriated by wealthy white landowners. "Sharecropping," History.com, Updated: June 7, 2019, https://www.history.com/topics/black-history/sharecropping

43. Knapp, 1969. op. cit., Chapter 3.

44. Knapp, 1969. op. cit., Chapter 4.

45. Knapp, 1973. op. cit., p. 21.

46. "Smith-Lever Act of 1914." Wikipedia, retrieved August 2020, http://en.wikipedia.org/wiki/Smith-Lever_Act_of_1914

47. "Farm Credit System," Wikipedia, retrieved August 2020, http://en.wikipedia.org/wiki/Farm_Credit_System#Authorization

48. Knapp, 1973, op. cit., p. 120.

49. Nadeau, op. cit., pp. 43-45.

50. Agricultural Cooperative Statistics 2016, USDA Rural Development, December 2017, https://www.rd.usda.gov/files/publications/SR80_CooperativeStatistics2016.pdf

51. Dave Grace and Associates, op. cit., p. 5,

52. Knapp, 1973. Op. cit., Chapters 16 and 17.

53. Ibid, p. 361.

54. Ibid, p. 373.

55. "Co-op facts and figures," NRECA, 2020, https://www.electric.coop/ wp-content/uploads/2020/06/Coop_FactsAndFigures_June2020.pdf

56. "History," Union Cab, retrieved August 2020, https://www.unioncab.com/ History

57. "2018 Annual Report," Mondragon Corporation, https://www.mondragon-corporation.com/wp-content/themes/mondragon/docs/eng/annual-report-2018.pdf

58. "New report highlights lessons from Mondragon - the world's largest worker co-op," Co-operatives UK, May 25, 2019, https://www.uk.coop/ newsroom/new-report-highlights-lessons-worlds-largest-worker-co-op

59. Ibid.

60. Note from Tom Webb, October 19, 2020.

61. "Overview: Worker Cooperatives," Community-wealth.org, retrieved August 2020, https://community-wealth.org/content/worker-cooperatives

62. Dave Grace and Associates, op. cit. p. 5.

63. "About our members," CICOPA, retrieved August 2020, https://www.cicopa. coop/about/our-members/

64. "What is Social Enterprise?" Social Enterprise, retrieved August 2020, https://socialenterprise.us/about/social-enterprise/

65. Borzaga, Carlo, and Defourny, Jacques, (eds.), *The Emergence of Social Enterprise*, Routledge, 2004, p. 171

66. Borzaga, C., Poledrini, S., & Galera, G., "Social Enterprise in Italy: Typology, Diffusion and Characteristics," Euricse Working Paper 96, 2017 https://www.euricse.eu/wp-content/uploads/2017/11/WP-96_17-ICSEM.pdf

67. Duda, John, "The Italian Region Where Co-ops Produce a Third of Its GDP," Yes Magazine, July 5, 2016, http://www.yesmagazine.org/new-economy/the-italian-place-where-co-ops-drive-the-economy-and-most-people-are-members-20160705

68. Borzaga, Carlo; Galera, Giulia; Franchini, Barbara; Chiomento, Stefania; Nogales, Rocío; and Carini, Chiara, Social enterprises and their ecosystems in Europe: Comparative synthesis report, European Commission, Luxembourg: Publications Office of the European Union, 2020, pp. 106-107, https://europa.eu/!Qq64ny.

69. Conaty, Pat, Social Cooperatives: a Democratic Co-production Agenda for Care Services in the UK, Co-operatives UK, 2014, p. 4, https://josswinn.org/wp-content/uploads/2014/12/CUK-Social-Co-operatives-Report-final.pdf

70. "Recent evolutions of the Social Economy in the European Union: Executive Summary," European Economic and Social Committee, 2017, http://unsse.org/wp-content/uploads/2017/08/CIRIEC-EESC-Executive-Summary-1.6.2017-1.pdf

71. "Cooperatives in social development, Report of the Secretary-General," United Nations General Assemby, July 17, 2017, http://undocs.org/A/72/159

72. Knapp, 1969, op. cit., Chapter IV.

73. Land-grant universities were established in 1862 by the U.S. federal government to teach "agriculture and the mechanic arts … Though the act specifically stated that other scientific and classical studies need not be excluded. https://www.britannica.com/topic/land-grant-university

74. https://europa.eu/european-union/about-eu/history_en

75. https://en.wikipedia.org/wiki/Cooperatives_Europe

76. A Brief Chronicle of the Modern Japanese Consumer Cooperative Movement, https: //community-wealth.org/sites/clone.community-wealth.org/files/downloads/book-saito.pdf; https://jccu.coop/eng/coop/history.html

77. Brief History of Japan Workers' Co-operative Union (JWCU), UN Department of Economic and Social Affairs, 2016, https://www.un.org/esa/socdev/egms/docs/2016/Coops-2030Agenda/Nakano2.pdf

78. http://www.icaap.coop/aboutus-ica-asia-pacific

79. https://icaafrica.coop/en/ica-africa

80. https://www.aciamericas.coop/Who-we-are

81. The National Cooperative Business Association was formed in 1917. The organization was originally called the Cooperative League of the USA (CLUSA). It is usually referred to today as NCBA CLUSA. I often use "CLUSA" to refer to the organization's international division.

82. https://nesawg.org/news/model-network-federation-of-southern-cooperatives

83. "Who is TCC," Tri-County Communications Cooperative," retrieved August 2020, https://tccpro.net/gettcc/about-us/

84. Rod Nisestuen was an innovative leader in the cooperative community not only in Wisconsin, but nationally. He led the Wisconsin Federation of Cooperatives for over 30 years and also played a leadership role in the National Cooperative Business Association. He received the Association's prestigious Cooperative Hall of Fame award in 2003. He served for almost eight years as the Secretary of the Wisconsin Department of Agriculture, Trade and Consumer Protection until his tragic death by drowning in 2010. Rod was my mentor and friend, and opened the door for me to a lifetime career in cooperatives.

85. This dual structure allowed the organization to simultaneously be a cooperative and also be able to receive tax-deductible donations and grants as a 501(c)(3) fund approved by the Internal Revenue Service.

86. These donors included CUNA (Credit Union National Association), CUNA Mutual, the National Cooperative Bank, Nationwide Insurance, The National Cooperative Business Association, Cooperative Development Foundation, and the Cooperative Foundation.

87. "Who we are," Columinate, retrieved August 2020, https://columinate.coop/who-we-are/

88. "Rural Cooperative Development Grant Program," SDA, 2020, https://www.rd.usda.gov/programs-services/rural-cooperative-development-grant-program

89. "About us," CooperationWorks!, retrieved August 2020, https://cooperationworks.coop/about/ (Note that the group was named after the book that David Thompson and I wrote in 1996 – with our wholehearted permission and support.)

90. "Who we are," CooperationWorks!, retrieved August 2020, https://cooperationworks.coop/about/#whoweare

91. "National Organic Program," Wikipedia, retrieved August 2020, http://en.wikipedia.org/wiki/National_Organic_Program

92. Duda, op. cit.

93. "Mission and values," NCBA CLUSA, https://ncbaclusa.coop/about-us/mission-and-values/

94. VOCA (Volunteers for Overseas Cooperative Development) merged with ACDI (Agricultural Cooperative Development International) in 1997, https://www.sourcewatch.org/index.php/ACDI/VOCA

95. One of the issues that provided an incentive for farmers to sell directly to trading companies was that by the end of the growing season, many of them had run out of food reserves and were desperate for ways to purchase food. Traders took advantage of this situation and purchased paprika and other agricultural products from these farmers at low prices. CLUSA could have initiated an early purchase program to counter this practice.

96. "Conservation Agriculture," FAO, retrieved August 2020, http://www.fao.
org/conservation-agriculture/overview/what-is-conservation-agriculture/en/

97. "Kwame Nkrumah," Wikipedia, retrieved August 2020, https://en.wikipedia.
org/wiki/Kwame_Nkrumah

98. "About Us," Kuapa Kokoo, retrieved August 2020, https://www.kuapakokoo.
com/index.php/about-us/

99. "The Divine Story," Divine Chocolate, retrieved August 2020 https://www.
divinechocolate.com/us/divine-story

100. Boakye, Albert Akwasi, Legal Framework Analysis Ghana National Report,
International Co-operative Alliance – Africa, November 2018, https://
coops4dev.coop/sites/default/files/2019-10/Ghana%20Legal%20Framework%20
Analysis%20Report_1.pdf

101. Guide to Cooperative Approaches to Community Health -Tools, Tips &
Lessons for Greater Participation and Sustainability of West African Health
Mutuals, USAID/CLUSA, 2009.

102. Abt Associates, https://www.abtassociates.com

103. Nadeau, E.G., "The First Mile: The Potential for Community-Based Health
Cooperatives in Developing Countries," The Cooperative Society Project,
2020, https://thecooperativesociety.org/wp-content/uploads/2020/02/12212-
the-first-mile-community-based-health-cooperatives-.pdf

104. Land O'Lakes is a large dairy cooperative based in the United States. It
has an international division that provides assistance to cooperatives in
developing countries. The international division changed its name in 2019
to Land O'Lakes Venture 37. In the book, I will refer to the division as Land
O'Lakes. https://www.landolakesventure37.org

105. Note from Todd Thompson, September 29, 2020.

106. Nadeau, E.G., and Ncwadi, Mpumelelo, "Strategies for Increasing
Black Commercial Farming in South Africa," September 2017, https://
thecooperativesociety.org/wp-content/uploads/2020/02/cdc3d-report_
strategies-for-increasing-black-farming-in-south-africa.pdf

107. Nadeau and Ncwadi, ibid.

108. "Aga Khan Foundation," retrieved August 2020, https://www.akdn.org/our-agencies/aga-khan-foundation

109. "Mozambique: PROMOTION OF CONSERVATION AGRICULTURE (PROMAC)," NCBA CLUSA, https://ncbaclusa.coop/project/promotion-of-conservation-agriculture-promac/; "Mozambique: Conservation Agriculture Promotion (PROMAC II)," NCBA CLUSA, https://ncbaclusa.coop/project/mozambique-conservation-agriculture-promotion-promac-ii/

110. "NCBA CLUSA celebrates Sam Filiaci's 40 years of service in Southeast Asia," NCBA CLUSA, October 28, 2019, https://ncbaclusa.coop/blog/ncba-clusa-celebrates-sam-filiacis-40-years-of-service-in-southeast-asia/

111. Ibid.

112. "Entrepreneurship," Business Dictionary, retrieved August 2020, http://www.businessdictionary.com/definition/entrepreneurship.html

113. Cooperatives in Development, Accessed November 2020, https://coopseurope.coop/development/welcome-cooperatives-international-development

114. "The ICA launches the International Cooperative Entrepreneurship Think Tank (ICETT)," International Cooperative Alliance, October 23, 2018, https://www.ica.coop/en/newsroom/news/ica-launches-international-cooperative-entrepreneurship-think-tank-icett

115. "17 Goals," United Nations, retrieved August 2020," https://sdgs.un.org/goals

116. "Transforming our world: A cooperative 2030, Cooperative contributions to SDG 7," COPAC and ICA, 2018, http://www.copac.coop/wp-content/uploads/2018/07/COPAC_TransformBrief_SDG7.pdf

117. Knapp, 1969 and 1973, op. cit.

118. World Co-op Monitor, Exploring the Cooperative Economy. Report 2019, Euricse and ICA, 2019, https://www.ccw.coop/uploads/Publications/World%20Co-op%20Monitor%202019.pdf

119. Technically, the international co-op data collection process was not a "census" because it did not involve the gathering of information directly from co-ops, but rather primarily relied on data aggregated by government co-op offices, co-op apex organizations, and other sources.

120. Dave Grace and Associates, op. cit.

121. Swanson, Walden, interview, March 13, 2015.

122. CoMetrics, 2020, https://www.cometrics.com

123. "Tackling Side Selling in Malt Barley Cooperatives," OCDC, 2019, https://www.ocdc.coop/wp-content/uploads/2019/01/Ethiopia_side_selling_overview_000.pdf

124. "About," Committee for the Promotion and Advancement of Cooperatives, http://www.copac.coop/about/

125. https://www.un.org/en/desa

126. "Coopedia Knowledge Base launched," Coops Europe, September 8, 2020, https://coopseurope.coop/resources/news/coopedia-knowledge-base-launched

127. https://coops4dev.coop/en/coops4dev

128. Agricultural Producer Organization (AgPrO) Training Modules, Global Innovations Exchange, accessed August 2020, https://www.globalinnovationexchange.org/resources/agricultural-producer-organization-agpro-training-modules

129. Enabling Cooperative Development, Principles for Legal Reform, OCDC, 2006, https://ocdc.coop/wp-content/uploads/2018/11/enabling_coop_dev_english.pdf

130. Creating CLARITY: Assessment, Analysis and Outreach for Cooperative Legal Reform, OCDC, 2009, https://ocdc.coop/wp-content/uploads/2018/11/creating_clarity_english.pdf

131. Applying the CLARITY Principles to the Nicaraguan Cooperative Law, OCDC, accessed August 2020, https://ocdc.coop/wp-content/uploads/2018/11/applying_clarity_english.pdf

132. Cooperative Advocacy: A Practical Guide to Cooperative Legal and Regulatory Reform, Clarity, 2013, http://www.clarity.coop/pdf/cooperative_advocacy_vol_4.pdf

133. "Introduction," ICA, accessed August 2020, https://www.ica.coop/en/welcome-webpage-ica-cooperative-law-committee-ica-clc

134. Henrÿ, Hagen, *Guidelines for Cooperative Legislation*, Third edition revised, ILO, 2012, https://www.ilo.org/wcmsp5/groups/public/---ed emp/---emp ent/documents/publication/wcms_195533.pdf

135. Blueprint for a Co-operative Decade, Chapter 4, NFCA, 2013, http://nfca.coop/wp-content/uploads/2011/12/ICA%20Blueprint%20for%20a%20Co-operative%20Decade.pdf

136. "Global Development Co-operative Fund," ICMIF, retrieved August 2020, https://www.icmif.org/tags/global-co-operative-development-fund

137. "Global Co-operative Impact Fund to provide funding for developing co-operatives," ICA, May 19, 2015, https://www.ica.coop/en/media/news/global-co-operative-impact-fund-provide-funding-developing-co-operatives

138. "CoopMed," retrieved August 2020, http://www.coopmed.eu/fund/

139. "Fundraising for the people and causes you care about," gofundme, accessed August 2020, https://www.gofundme.com/?utm_source=google&utm medium=cpc&utm_campaign=US_GoFundMe_EN_Exact_Desktop NewDormant_Core&utm_content=gofundme&utm_term=gofundme_e_c_ad&gclid=CjwKCAjwydP5BRBREiwA-qrCGr1NLsrDglymUjXlw5PLvBp5UBtsd89WC NFIga1AfgnEOQblP39hrBoCT2IQAvD BwE

140. https://coopseurope.coop/development/about/who-we-are

141. https://canada.coop/en/programs/co-op-development/international-co-operative-development

142. "Cooperative Identity, values and principles," ICA, retrieved August 2020, https://www.ica.coop/en/cooperatives/cooperative-identity

143. https://coopseurope.coop/development/

144. Nadeau, E.G., "Co-op to Co-op Trade: Linking Smallholder Producer Co-ops in Developing Countries with Consumer Co-ops in Developed Countries," OCDC, 2013, https://thecooperativesociety.org/wp-content/uploads/2021/02/Co-op-to-Co-op-Trade-White-Paper.pdf

145. "17 Goals," op. cit.

146. Dave Grace and Associates, op. cit.

147. https://www.ilo.org/global/topics/cooperatives/areas-of-work/lang--en/index.htm

148. "Climate Change Impacts," NOAA, February 2019, https://www.noaa.gov/education/resource-collections/climate/climate-change-impacts

149. Nadeau, E.G., "Community Solar Cooperatives in Developing Countries," The Cooperative Society, May 2019, https://thecooperativesociety.org/wp-content/uploads/2020/09/190328-Community-solar-cooperatives.pdf

150. The Paris Agreement, United Nations Climate Change, 2018. https://unfccc.int/process-and-meetings/the-paris-agreement/the-paris-agreement

151. "Ensure access to affordable, reliable, sustainable and modern energy," United Nations Sustainable Development Goals, 2015, https://www.un.org/sustainabledevelopment/energy/

152. "Universal energy access by 2030 is now within reach thanks to growing political will and falling costs," International Energy Agency, October 2017, https://www.iea.org/news/universal-energy-access-by-2030-is-now-within-reach-thanks-to-growing-political-will-and-falling-costs

153. "State of the Global Mini-Grids Market 2020 Report," BloombergNEF, June 2020, https://www.seforall.org/system/files/2020-06/MGP-2020-SEforALL.pdf

154. Chapa, Sergio, "Solar microgrid designed in Texas Hill Country deployed in West Africa," SanAntonio Business Journal, June 27, 2018, https://www.bizjournals.com/sanantonio/news/2018/06/27/solar-microgrid-designed-in-texas-hill-country.html

155. See, for example: Richardson, Jake, "Kenyan Electrification Plan Could Achieve Universal Access By 2022," Clean Technica, January 15, 2019, https://cleantechnica.com/2019/01/15/kenyan-electrification-plan-could-achieve-universalaccess-by-2022/; "Kenya Launches Ambitious Plan to Provide Electricity to All Citizens by 2022, World Bank, December 6, 2018, https://www.worldbank.org/en/news/press-release/2018/12/06/kenya-launches-ambitiousplan-to-provide-electricity-to-all-citizens-by-2022; "Boosting Access to Electricity in Africa through Innovation, Better Regulation," World Bank, https://www.worldbank.org/en/region/afr/publication/boosting-access-to-electricity-inafrica-through-innovation-better-regulation

156. Richardson, Jake, "Home Solar Lighting Systems Come To Kenya From Azuri & Unilever," Clean Technica, December 19, 2018, https://cleantechnica.com/2018/12/19/home-solar-lighting-systems-come-to-kenya-fromazuri-unilever/

157. Lavrushko, Olga, "Ensuring the 'lungs of the planet' keep us alive: 5 things you need to know about forests and the UN," 10 May 2019, https://news.un.org/en/story/2019/05/1038291

158. Nadeau, E.G., and Nadeau, Luc, "The Role of Forestry Cooperatives in Climate Change Mitigation," March 2016, https://thecooperativesociety.org/wp-content/uploads/2020/02/237e5-the-role-of-forestry-cooperatives-in-climate-change-mitigation.pdf

159. FAO (2010) "Global Forest Resources Assessment 2010," http://www.fao.org/docrep/013/i1757e/i1757e.pdf.

160. "A World of Opportunity: The World's Forests from a Restoration Perspective" (2011), http://www.profor.info/profor/sites/profor.info/files/Landscapes-Opportunity21Jan11.pdf.

161. UN-REDD Programme, "About REDD+," https://www.unredd.net/about/what-is-redd-plus.html

162. FAO (2010), op. cit.

163. FAO (2007) "The state of food and agriculture" http://www.fao.org/3/a-a1200e.pdf

164. The Katoomba Group (2008) "Payment for Ecosystem Services: A Primer" Forest Trends, The Katoomba Group and UNEP.

165. For example, Digby, Margaret, and Edwardson, T.E., (1976), "The organisation of forestry co-operatives," Occasional paper - Plunkett Foundation for Co-operative Studies; no. 41.

166. This paper uses the phrase "forestry cooperative" to connote a broad array of locally based, forestry-related organizations. Not all of them are registered as cooperatives nor do they all subscribe to the seven cooperative principles, but most share the basic definition of a cooperative: an organization that is owned and democratically controlled by the people who use its services.

167. For example, World Resources Institute (2008), "Success Rate of Community Forest Management (CFM) in 49 Countries Studied," https://www.wri.org/resources/charts-graphs/success-rate-community-forest-management-cfm-49-countries-studied

168. https://www.un-redd.org

169. Nadeau, E.G., 2020, op. cit.

170. The program was carried out from 2001 to 2012 by CLUSA, a division of the U.S.-based National Cooperative Business Association, and funded by the U.S. Agency for International Development.

171. For example, International Conference on Global Health, 2008: http://www.globalhealth.org/conference/view_top.php3?id=845; USAID Deliver Project: https://deliver.jsi.com

172. The author hypothesizes that the community-based health cooperative model would also be effective in poor urban neighborhoods. However, because the Kenya program on which this model is based is a rural one, the focus of this paper is on the application of the model in rural areas.

173. At the present time, these associations are not legally structured as cooperatives. However, they generally operate under the same principles as co-ops: voluntary and open membership, democratic member control, member economic participation, autonomy and independence, education and training, cooperation with other health associations, and concern for community.

174. https://www.gatesfoundation.org

175. "Cooperative identity, values & principles," International Cooperative Alliance, https://www.ica.coop/en/cooperatives/cooperative-identity

176. See p. 32.

177. Nadeau, E.G., and Thompson, David J., *Cooperation Works!*: How People Are Using Cooperative Action to Rebuild Communities and Revitalize the Economy, Lone Oak Press, June 1, 1997.

178. https://thecooperativesociety.org